Dear Lisa

*My Inner Children
taught me how to
love myself*

Anji Marsh

Copyright © 2021 by Anji Marsh

All rights reserved. No part of this publication may be reproduced, distributed, or transmitted in any form or by any means, including photocopying, recording, or other electronic or mechanical methods, without the prior written permission of the publisher, except in the case of brief quotations embodied in critical reviews and certain other noncommercial uses permitted by copyright law.

Book Design by HMDpublishing

Names and identities in this book have been changed to protect the privacy of those mentioned

Dedication
For my son, Tom
My greatest blessing
X

Contents

Preface 7

Dear Lisa 9
14th May 2020

Our Friendship 15
19th May 2020

My Inner Children 19
21st May 2020

Not Okay 27
26th May 2020

Triggers 33
28th May 2020

My Three Marriages 35
29th May 2020

The Abuse 52
1st June 2020

David 60
2nd June 2020

Protecting Children 73
8th June 2020

Breast Cancer 79
9th June 2020

Enough Time 95
19th June 2020

Counselling 101
22nd June 2020

Home with ABANDONED 103
14th July 2020

Perception 115
24th July 2020

Alone 120
27th August 2020

I am enough 122
23rd September 2020

Inner Strength 128
6th October 2020

Letter about David 132
10th October 2020

Progress 136
24th October 2020

Back at David's House 138
16th November 2020

Self-Care 140
19th November 2020

My Career 149
20th November 2020

Bye for Now 155
21st November 2020

SELF-HELP GUIDE 159
Introduction 160
Playmates/Counterparts 162
Spiritual Laws 164
No Outside Fix 169
Pain and Fear 171
Wise Inner Parent 174
Self-Care Toolbox 176
Journaling 178
It's Okay Not to Feel Okay 179
Final Note 181
Acknowledgments 182
Resources 184

Preface

Lisa was a close friend of mine for most of my life. We wrote to each other regularly, staying in close contact and maintaining an active friendship. But fourteen years ago, we reluctantly lost touch. My desire to write to Lisa again has, however, encouraged me to write this book.

One day, after feeling stressed, I was thinking about how simple life seemed years ago and I reflected on how Lisa and I wrote to each other. Initially, I started writing the letter as a way for me to express myself. However, I have for some time, wanted to express my knowledge to support other people, too.

You will see as you read through the letter, my confusion at the start and my clarity towards the end. Writing it has opened my eyes to seeing more of *me*. I have learnt how to support myself and realised that what I needed all along was ME. I just wasn't seeing how to do that, even though I was telling myself what I needed. Now that *I* know, I hope *you* will be able to know how to be there for yourself, too.

The first part of this book is my letter to Lisa, which is about the trauma I have experienced in my life. It shows the damage these experiences caused that prevented me from looking after myself in cer-

Dear Lisa

tain areas of my life. However, eventually I realised I needed to acknowledge my uncomfortable feelings and so set out on a journey of discovering my Inner Children. This discovery showed me how to support myself each day in a way that meets my needs with each moment. I am much more accepting of how my life is right now, because I know NOW is all I have. Life, whether an easy day or a more difficult one, is *this* day of my life. Now I know so much more about how to look after myself in whatever is present in each day.

The second part of this book is a Self-Help Guide. This section contains the tools which I talk about in the letter and have used for myself. You will gain more understanding from the Self-Help Guide by reading the letter and seeing how I have applied this in my life.

The book highlights that you are not broken and don't need fixing, but instead, you just need LOVE. You receive the love you need by giving LOVING ATTENTION to all parts of yourself: this is how you love yourself.

I hope you enjoy discovering your inner children as you read through the book and develop an understanding of what they say to you. I love discovering mine and continue to love them all. Even when the most painful, hurting ones appear, I still feel connected to the strong ones. I know how to help them now.

My journey goes on as my life continues. I don't know the ups and downs ahead but I do know, whichever way things fall, that it doesn't really matter. All that does matter is being there for myself and giving me the loving attention that I need.

Anji Marsh

Dear Lisa

14th May 2020

Wow! The strangest thing just happened: For about a week now, I've been thinking about writing you a letter, a very long letter, and today, Facebook has suggested you as a friend.

I didn't think I'd have sent the letter in all honesty, because I may not even have been able to find you. Basically, it would have started with, *"Sorry"* and then gone on to tell you all that has happened to me, what I've discovered about myself, why I behaved the way I did and how you were the best friend I ever had.

I sense you're happy and well; I really hope you are, because you deserve to be.

You were a good part of my life.

Lisa, I wrote the above as a message to you on Messenger, on the 23rd of April 2020. I know you haven't seen it. I could send you a friend request of course, but I'm not sure you would welcome that. So,

Dear Lisa

I've decided to begin this letter to you because Facebook never sends me suggested friend notifications and I, therefore, feel this is a sign to write to you. You may never read it, but I need to write it, nonetheless.

You may wonder why I feel the need to write to you now, after so long. I've had a lot of stress and as I'm currently not working due to the Coronavirus pandemic, it's given me space to think and reflect on things. Not being able to go anywhere has made me reflect on how life was years ago. It seemed so simple thirty years ago. We didn't have Facebook, Twitter and all the many other ways of sharing every part of our waking life. Everything seems so invasive nowadays and much more complicated. Technology may benefit us in many ways, but I think it's destructive in many others.

Anyway, I started thinking about how we used to write to each other. Do you remember? Every week I wrote a letter to you and every week you wrote back to me. We did that for years. Looking back, that makes me realise just how much a part of each other's lives we were.

I remember how upset you were when I went to Australia; you didn't know if I would return. Seven months later, I was back. Every day, as I travelled around Australia, I wrote to you, telling you everything I was doing. If you still have those letters, you'll have the only step-by-step account of that trip. I'd love to read them. I'm now feeling quite emotional thinking about the bond between us and how writing to you made me feel close to you. You really did travel every step of the way with me. That was twenty eight years ago, can you believe it? I'll always know how long ago it was because when I came home in

Dear Lisa

the summer of 1992, I became pregnant. Tom was born in May 1993 and he's just turned twenty-seven.

If I remember correctly, our friendship fell apart about eighteen years ago. However, we did have contact up until about fourteen years ago, where we spoke on the phone.

I don't really know where to begin. Do I start with why our friendship ended? I could tell you about the child abuse I suffered and how much that affected me, about how I survived it yet often feel as though I'm falling apart. I have so much to tell you about what I've been discovering about myself. I could begin with my failed marriages and how I once again endured an abusive relationship through no fault of my own.

I *can* tell you that I wasn't capable of protecting myself. I didn't know how to look after myself, how to respect myself and how to say "no". I've had counselling and I can protect myself now, however. I respect myself like I've never done before. It doesn't come easy though, because deep inside me, I trust people to look after me, yet all too often they're just thinking about themselves and what THEY want. At least now I can protect myself so much better and I don't give myself away anymore.

Lisa, you probably think that doesn't sound like me. I know my friends see me as a strong and focused woman, capable and in control of my life and of achieving. Well, that's how I survived, with control and the need for stability. I was like that because I believed that nobody would really look after me or was truly there for me. So, I had no option but to be there for myself. That made me capable, self-reliant and self-sufficient. Although I still have that be-

Dear Lisa

lief, I'm trying to see that there are people who do look after me and are there for me, even if at times it doesn't feel like it. I had cancer four years ago and going through that made me see that people *are* there for me, especially when I really need them.

I do have that strong side, but I often feel incredibly sad and realise I'm not okay. I've thought about suicide so many times, and my life seems to get harder as I get older. I think it's because I have more time. My brain was distracted when I was younger, whilst focusing on my three-year goals. I focused on my career, then my child and family life, then moving and starting my own business. I don't know. It just seems all I've kept inside of me is now surfacing and much of that is because I become very emotionally triggered by my current boyfriend, David. I run away often, as in, I retreat back to my own space and need time out, but we always get back together. It's been a continuous cycle for about six years now.

I go to a ladies' group twice a month in Norwich, with the Sue Lambert Trust. It's for women who have been sexually abused. It's really helping me to understand a lot about the effects of the abuse, and it helps me being with other women who have been through similar experiences. It can be upsetting at times, because it's never nice to hear how someone has suffered. All the women there are so lovely. They're loving, kind and caring people and it's so sad that they have been mistreated, manipulated and abused.

I keep in touch with some of the ladies so we can support each other when needed. Hearing people feel the same as I do really helps. It's a great group because it's given me a voice without being judged.

Dear Lisa

When I hear how some of the women haven't always survived by making healthy choices, I don't think badly of them; I feel compassion and see how none of it was *their* fault. This helps me because I judge myself. I often feel like a bad person and that I've messed up. If I can see it's not their fault, then it helps me to see I, too, wasn't to blame.

The hardest thing is what I've done as an adult, because I *am* an adult and feel I should know better. I do know and now see that because I was unable to protect myself and had little self-respect, I engaged in unhealthy activities. It's a real struggle in my mind to be "okay" with all that has happened. All of it has been through the direct actions of the significant people in my life and them not looking after me, but instead putting me in hurtful situations. That will never happen again, because I can now protect myself. It hurts so much to know that I haven't been looked after and protected. I wish you were here and I was telling you this face-to-face. I wish you could hug me as I cry. I miss you, Lisa.

I seem to be on a roller coaster of feeling okay then not, where I become easily triggered, emotionally. When I feel like this, I find myself releasing a lot of anger and frustration, which I've been carrying for years. I would never have thought of myself as an angry person. But I now feel what I've done is to hold on to so much that has hurt me that it now all needs to be released. I don't walk around being angry. I'm still a very positive person. However, the communication I have with David, at times, really frustrates me and also makes me realise the damage that's been caused by the things that have happened to me.

Dear Lisa

I'm also suffering with a swollen abdomen at the moment. I'm going to the doctor on Friday for blood tests and an examination. Hopefully, that's nothing to worry about, although I can't help having some thoughts about cancer.

My mum's breast cancer spread to her liver. I know my breast cancer has been treated and I doubt very much I have cancer now. I was diagnosed at forty seven, which was the same age that my mum died. You probably remember that.

I can recall spending the Christmas after my mum passed away in February of that year, with you and your husband, Gary, in Chippenham. I remember wanting to do something different that year to make the first Christmas without her easier. I think the firsts of everything are the hardest after someone has died. You're the only friend I've ever spent a Christmas with and that was thirty years ago. Wow! Thirty years.

Writing this now feels like it used to when I would write to you from Australia. I could only send letters and not receive any back until I returned to my aunt and uncle's house in Townsville. So, this again, is a one-way letter, and the difference now is that I can't send it because I don't have your address. I do believe you may live somewhere in, or near Carlisle, though.

And now, after wondering what to start telling you, I've decided to begin with why our friendship fell apart...

Our Friendship

19th May 2020

Our friendship falling apart had nothing to do with you. I actually can't remember all the finer details, but I do remember enough to explain. You may remember what I told you at the time, too.

I was with James, my second husband. What I didn't realise at the time, was that my marriage was actually falling apart. You and Gary came to visit us and stayed for a few days. You and I went dancing in a nightclub in Norwich. I can't remember the evening very well, but maybe you can? I think I had some interest from a younger man whom I danced with.

Anyway, it was this particular weekend that Gary came upstairs whilst I was in my bathroom and made a pass at me. I handled it really badly. As I explained earlier, it was in the days where I didn't respect myself or look after myself. I've come to realise since, that in *not* looking after myself, I didn't look after you either. I look back now and even though I wasn't capable then of what I am now, I *am* truly sorry that I let you down. It deeply upsets me and I wish I could go back to that time and respond differently.

James and I were in an open relationship back then, which was something else that did me immense harm, mentally and emotionally. It was because of this, I told James that Gary had kissed me. I can't remember the conversation with you then, but I know the content was about all four of us doing something together in a sexual capacity. I can't remember why that never happened, but I know now that I'm very glad it didn't. What I do remember, however, is speaking to you on the phone about Gary kissing me. It obviously wasn't an easy or positive conversation.

Telling you what happened caused problems in your marriage, or maybe it was the straw that broke the camel's back for you and Gary. It was after this that things were no longer the same between us. We didn't have any contact for a long while, then a few years later, you contacted me again.

There's so much I don't know and so little I remember about what happened to you after that. I know you got divorced and I think I remember things being really horrible for you. I think you even lost custody of your daughter. I can't imagine how that must have been for you. All those years of desperately trying to have a child and then later in her little life, she can't be with you. I hope she is a part of your life now and you have the most wonderful

Our Friendship

mother-daughter relationship. I think that Gary had cancer and I don't know if he's still alive or not. If you ever wanted to tell me what you went through, I would be so willing to listen.

I remember a little more of the last contact we had. You were in a relationship where you didn't seem happy and your boyfriend wanted to share you with other men. I can recall speaking to you on the phone. I was in York, walking around the shops with Peter, my third husband. I remember experiencing the feeling of concern for you, knowing that you weren't okay. Peter was also concerned, which is ironic, because this is the reason my third marriage ended.

Lisa, I'm so sorry I didn't look after you. I'm so sorry I wasn't there for you.

I look back at all the mistakes I've made in my adult life and each one has been a reactive response. By that, I mean I didn't take the first action, never had a desire to do something, but my reaction to what others did was my downfall.

It's through the counselling I had and what happened in my marriage with Peter, that taught me I wasn't able to protect myself and allowed others to take a piece of me. My counsellor taught me one very important thing: I am precious. This was an eye-opening moment that took me back, right through to my childhood. I wasn't treated as precious then, or indeed by many others since. But I always feel precious with David. I feel very safe with him in that way. I feel precious and pure as if nothing has ever happened to me before. However, I often feel upset a lot of the time, especially when my emotions are triggered.

Dear Lisa

Being in the relationship with David and having the emotional upset has allowed me to discover many of my inner children. The way David behaves has caused a lot to surface within me, which is a reason I felt I needed to attend the group at the Sue Lambert Trust.

My Inner Children

21st May 2020

It's a beautiful day; very warm. I've been feeling a lot more relaxed over the last few days. I think writing this letter to you is helping me.

My relationship with David has uncovered many of my inner children. Most people have heard of the inner child, but we have lots of them. Even though I know this because of my work, it's often easier to see and help others than it is to see and help yourself. Having said that, however, I think if I didn't have the understanding and knowledge that I do have about all of this, I don't think I would have been able to carry on as I have, because it's not been easy at times.

I've felt so low, but my understanding and knowledge has really helped me to be able to help myself. I'm able to recognise my inner children and I'm learning how to be there for me. This is still an ongoing process and probably will be for the rest of my life, but I've discovered so many parts of myself: their names and behaviours and what they so desperately need. The behaviours are just a way of getting what is lacking.

This obviously isn't unique to me, as everyone acts from their inner child at some point. It's what happens so often in relationships. In fact, relationships are the perfect place to get to know your inner children, because two people that come together will be a mirror for each other. This is crucially what has happened in my relationship with David, more than it ever has before.

So many times, I find myself running away because I can't bear the pain. And when that pain eventually subsides, I'm happy with David again. Don't get me wrong, he's not a horrible man and he does love me very much, but the way he behaves causes my inner children to appear. Our biggest difference is that he's much more laid back than I am, with his favourite phrase being, "Something will happen".

Well, that's difficult for me because I believe it's up to *me* to make things happen. I'm a very organised person. I'm always responsible and conscious of what I should be prioritising. The adult part of me is well developed. David, to me, seems like an eighteen year old. He's actually forty three; forty four next week, which makes me just over eight years older than him.

Over the seven years I've known him, I've actually lost count of how many times we've broken up. At first, I thought a lot of the problem was because of his financial situation and debt. But as time went

My Inner Children

on and that situation improved, the problems still remained. Basically, every situation that occurs just makes me feel unimportant, not good enough, unworthy and the complete opposite to what he feels about me. He gets frustrated and doesn't understand why I can't see how much I mean to him and how much he loves me. I know why: it's because I see the choices he makes or the words he uses. My brain hears, *"I'm not important, I'm not good enough,"* and then I feel neglected. There are things that David has had to be more responsible over, for example looking deeper at what's important and having to grow up more, basically. However, I feel my reaction is caused because of my past and the hurt I carry inside of me.

So, I'll introduce you to some of my inner children, the ones I've got to know more recently.

The first one I started to acknowledge was **SADNESS**. I suppose it wasn't hard to see her, as I spent so much time crying. The more I cried, the more I saw I had a very, very sad part of myself. Initially, I was just aware of **SADNESS** and just accepted she wasn't happy about what was happening at the time.

I've always been fairly good at allowing my emotions to be present. To me, that has always felt quite normal and part of being human. That's not to say that I didn't particularly like it. Obviously, if I'm crying, then I'm hurt in some way and that's never going to feel comfortable or okay. I've learnt so much more about how to be okay when *not* feeling okay. I know my uncomfortable feelings won't last, but instead, I know they're just present at this time.

Over time, I realised that my resilience and ability to be okay again was because I have a good connection to the positive parts of myself. This is where many people become swathed in depression, feeling down, negative and unable to cope. They don't have a good connection to positive aspects of themselves and they fight the uncomfortable feelings that are present, trying to suppress them in some way.

I often say, "It's not the presence of what feels bad that's the problem, but the absence of what feels good that is."

So, I've been able to allow **SADNESS** to be present, even though that feels painful, and I've used **HAPPINESS** to help her. I call it having playmates because all children like to have friends. It's like every aspect having a counterpart. In life, we are never meant to be alone, so why should parts of ourselves be on their own? I believe they are not. What this all means is that I'm learning to be there for myself. I was unable to be there for myself as a child. Children aren't capable of doing that. They should be looked after, protected and guided in a safe environment to enable them to grow into balanced, capable adults.

Now I *am* an adult and can be there for myself. I can protect myself, love myself and give myself all the loving attention I need. That may sound straightforward, but it's definitely easier said than done. I understood more about **SADNESS** as I discovered more of my inner children. I began to see how they work together and how several of them are present at the same time.

The next inner child I discovered was **SUFFERING**.

I recognised **SUFFERING** one day when I was feeling particularly distraught. I was feeling consumed by all the horrible experiences I'd had in my

My Inner Children

life. This introduced me to **SUFFERING**, a part of me that is carrying around all of the traumatic experiences I've endured. I felt I needed to draw her, so I did. She has an oversized bag on her back which contains all my suffering, and I thought, *"Wow! What an amazing part of me **SUFFERING** is."* She carries all this around with her, for ME. With all of the old suffering and any new suffering, her bag is able to hold it all. I saw what an incredibly strong part of me that is. Can you imagine where I'd be without her?

We are so often taught to let go of these things, these parts, like baggage is a bad thing. Well, I say, this part of who I am helps me. All parts hold great value; we just have to see the value they hold. I would not be able to function without this part holding all the suffering I've experienced. I'm truly grateful to her. I feel she has a very difficult job, but boy, she does it incredibly well.

I realised, when I discovered **SUFFERING**, that **SADNESS** cries for her. **SUFFERING** doesn't cry because she's too busy being strong. **SUFFERING** has a counterpart called **SURVIVAL**, and as they work in harmony, it enables me to survive and carry on with my life.

As time went on, I started to discover these parts of myself. I tried really hard not to run away from David whenever I became emotionally triggered. Last year, in 2019, I stayed with him for a much longer period of time that being around eight months rather than the usual three, and because I stayed longer, I discovered another inner child. This new inner child was a great discovery. Seeing her made me realise all of my failings from the past with regards to men. As soon as I saw her, all those parts of my life flashed before me. It felt like I saw my life from now, being rewound all the way back to my childhood. I saw all my failings and most importantly, I saw *why* I had failed. This inner child is called **NEGLECTED**.

NEGLECTED surfaced because I didn't run away from David. The longer I stayed the more neglected I felt. However, the feeling was so much more than that. When **NEGLECTED** is present, normally **UNIMPORTANT** and **UNLOVED** are present, too. I've realised **NEGLECTED** seeks loving attention. She takes it upon herself to make **UNIMPORTANT** and **UNLOVED** feel better. She yearns to help them, which makes her feel seen and present again.

The problem was that **NEGLECTED** didn't have the right skills to do this without causing more problems. She was definitely missing her playmate, her counterpart. Unfortunately, her solutions became a short-term fix, which just added more pain in the long run. What **NEGLECTED** needed was a loving mother to keep her safe and give to her the love and attention which came with respect, worth and value.

You see, my problem was the lack of the positive, of self-respect, self-worth and self-value. If I'd had those, I would have done things very differently. I would have been able to look after our friendship and I would have been able to say "no". I'm so incredibly grateful that I discovered **NEGLECTED** because seeing her has caused a huge shift in my ability to seek healthy attention.

You see, **NEGLECTED** surfaced because I needed more attention from David. I did get some, but he was allowing other things to get in the way when

My Inner Children

it was our time together, which then resulted in me feeling neglected.

I find it hard to simply just say or ask for what I want. I'm sure most of the time he would give me what I wanted, but I become upset when he isn't fully focused on me. I feel he should make the most of our time together without me having to ask.

Once I'm emotionally triggered and my inner children present themselves, all rationality goes. He's then presented with very stroppy children, and of course, he doesn't know how to deal with that. He becomes defensive and brings his own inner children out. This then escalates out of hand, resulting in an argument.

It's when this happens that I feel completely alone and unseen. I'm hurting and I need him to see my pain, but he doesn't. He just gets caught up in himself, and I can't cope with that reaction. Even though I blame him at the time, I don't blame him on the whole. I'd never expect him not to get triggered, too. I just *wish* he didn't and that he could see I'm not okay. I'm saying I need him and I need him to be there for me.

David giving attention to something else has triggered my uncomfortable feelings, but I know my reaction is from something deeper-rooted about my own experiences. My inner children still need that loving attention. I know it's not *his* job to heal me; it's mine. I also know it's me that needs to be there for myself and that's something I'm really working on.

Anyway, towards the end of last year, when feeling neglected, I had two men very willing to give me attention. I saw that maybe I'd have a way out from all

Dear Lisa

this pain that gets triggered with David. I so wanted someone to look after me properly.

I came extremely close to giving myself away. Thankfully, because I've now developed **SELF-RE-SPECT** and can look after myself so much better, I was able to see sense. I actually think it would destroy me now to give myself away sexually before falling in love with someone. I felt so bad. It really scared me that I came so close to doing something I would deeply regret, for myself and, of course, for David, too.

I'm glad, though, that this happened. It made me realise so much and that was when I discovered **NE-GLECTED**. I told David all about it. He was very supportive and listened to how **NEGLECTED** was so desperate for loving attention. And that's the key: loving attention. Unfortunately, **NEGLECTED** mistook 'sexual attention' for 'loving attention'.

There have been many unhealthy experiences of which **NEGLECTED** got me into, in my search for wanting to feel loved and wanted. Now, she has her counterpart, a loving and caring mother, to help her choose wisely.

Not Okay

26th May 2020

The bank holiday weekend has just passed. The weekend started on Friday for me, as I had an appointment with my doctor for my swollen tummy. I'm now waiting for the results of the blood tests and an appointment for a scan, as my bowel seems a bit full. It's feeling quite uncomfortable today which upsets me a bit. Hopefully I'll get the scan soon and will find out what's going on.

The weekend had a few stresses which led me to send David an email:

"David,

I am writing to you about all the times I get upset. It never actually matters what I'm upset about. What matters is that you see I'm not okay.

You say to me that you need me. Well, I need you, too. I need you to be there for me. You can help others to be okay, so why can't you help me? Why can't you see I'm not okay? That's what I need. You can then reassure me that things are okay in a gentle, kind, and nurturing way. I know you do that after I'm upset but it's too late then; the damage has been caused.

Can you not see that for my whole life I've been surviving alone? I have been there and still am, looking after everyone else to meet their needs. I want the same: for you to look after me and be there for me and to help me when I am upset.

The scar on my arm is a symbol. It says: "Please Help Me." I don't want to feel all these things, to feel pain and still be alone with it all. For years I was alone with the most horrible things that I couldn't tell anyone, never having anyone there to make it better for me. I had no one protecting me and giving me a safe space to tell all my darkest fears. Now, when those fears come out, I still don't have a safe place to express them.

You know, I can hardly bear the hurt of being so alone with the pain I feel and having nobody there to help. I want you to see my pain and to be held in your loving arms. Please be there for me; it's what I need. I love you and want to be okay with you."

So, that's what I sent him. He understood what I was trying to say whilst reading it, but the problem is, putting it into action.

I know this is a common problem in relationships. Life would be more harmonious if there was an understanding of why people behave the way they do. My reaction to something David does, which is actually okay, or not harming me in any way, is caused by a memory, a trauma or a belief which has been created in the past. So now, the situation doesn't feel safe because it has made me feel insecure in some way.

Not Okay

My reaction is to be unhappy, angry or upset with David, and then he becomes defensive. This is where it gets out of hand and I end up feeling terrible. I need him to realise and see that I'm hurting, rather than setting out to fight his own corner. I know that's difficult because he knows the reality of his actions.

At these times, there's nothing wrong with his actions, but at other times, there is. Either way, I'm upset and feel hurt. It doesn't actually matter to me what caused the reaction. What matters is the acknowledgment of how I feel. I either want reassurance or I want us to be a team to do things better.

Sometimes, I feel like I know what I'm doing and have the answers, and then at other times, I feel like I haven't got a clue. You hear stories of people that struggled to hold their life together and then overcome the things that happened to them. They feel empowered and turn their lives around. Well, I feel the opposite. I feel like I started my life strong, focused and together. Yet now, I often feel like I'm falling apart.

The only time I seem to feel settled is when I'm on my own, being single. I don't know if David is just the wrong man for me, or if I will ever feel settled with anyone. I've spent time with different men during the times I've broken up with David. I haven't felt any of them to be right for me, to want to have a relationship with.

I find it harder now that I respect myself and don't give myself away. It seems to me that men don't want to get to know a woman before being intimate with her. It's probably why so many relationships fail, because they started with a physical connection before moving on to an emotional one. They don't give themselves enough time to work out whether they actually like each other and are compatible to be together.

I want to spend time with someone. I want to fall in love with them because of our connection and how we treat each other. I only ever want to give myself to someone who loves me and whom I love in return. Men don't seem to have the patience needed to develop this bond. I want to spend time together, have fun and grow closer to each other. They just want to kiss me at the first opportunity.

This, once again, is people thinking what they want and putting their own desire before another. I don't think that's acceptable. Why would they think it is? If they remove their own desire, they can tell whether or not I want the same. If unsure, they could just ask.

I sometimes think, maybe the universe is testing me to make sure I'm looking after myself. At first, it was a good thing because I needed the practice in saying no. After a while I just thought, *"Enough is enough"*.

The questions I ask myself now are, should I be alone, have my friends and be in my safe little bubble, or do I stay with David and work through what surfaces?

On my own, my emotions aren't triggered like they are when I'm with David. I feel that means I don't get the opportunity to help myself. It's painful to keep having my emotions triggered, but he continues to love me through everything.

I spoke to him a little while ago. He's working today and he rang to see if I was happy. He so wants me to be happy. I know he really hates it when I'm not. I tend to forget that when I'm stressed, it affects him, too. It doesn't help when we are both stressed.

I do sometimes think I expect too much from him, and I get more stressed when he doesn't get it right. I obviously realise he can't always get it right, especially if he doesn't have the skill or knowledge, and actually, even *with* the skill and knowledge, I don't always get it right.

It's funny really, because I ask David to be gentle, kind and there for me and I know that means it's what I need to do with myself. I do that with myself in many ways, but I feel I need to do it more. I need to realise I *am* okay and I'm learning how to look after myself more when I'm not.

I think a lot of my focus is on helping other people. I find it really hard to be the person who is just receiving the help. Maybe that's the control I needed which has been my protection. The outer shell, strong and confident, always presents itself, and I'm sure that's why I've never really received the help I needed.

Whenever I've gone to a professional, they see the confident togetherness of my life sitting before them. There's nothing wrong with me on the outside, which is interesting really because normally, what's on the inside is manifested on the outside.

It's clear I have a strong, capable, self-reliant part of me which shows, but the inside of where I'm not okay shows, too. The professionals haven't looked in the right place to see it. They needed to look at the connection I had with my family and relationships, which perhaps didn't look too bad if you compare that to many of the dysfunctional relationships out there.

We all handle things in different ways. My way was the need for order and for everything to be stable. Luckily, it wasn't drink or drugs or anything like that. I suppose my need for order is the exact opposite of what drinking or drugs would create. I've never even been drunk because, basically, I don't trust anyone enough to make sure I'd be safe.

This is probably the very problem I have: trusting someone enough to really be there for me. In fact, I'm constantly proving to myself that people aren't. Poor David, he's doomed for failure with having to constantly prove he's capable of looking after me. Once again, I know that's *my* job and the question is, why am I not trusting myself? That will take some thought and there are probably quite a few answers to that question, too.

My business name is, **"Self Transformation"**, because it's about empowering people to be there for themselves, to realise they have the power to make any changes to their life and well-being, albeit with support. Support can help them learn to love and do things for themselves. Support is so important and it's something I have had to learn myself. It's been easier to support myself whilst harder to receive support from other people. That's another of the reasons why I went to the group at the Sue Lambert Trust.

Triggers

28th May 2020

I didn't write yesterday as I didn't feel very well. My tummy was very uncomfortable but the worse thing I felt was tiredness. So, I mainly rested and then went out for an evening walk when David came home. I'm feeling better today and less tired. I'm actually feeling a bit brighter, too.

I spoke to David, after writing to you on Tuesday, about him seeing and understanding that he just triggers things in me which are not always his fault but caused from the past. He does understand. I just hope he can remember if and when I'm emotionally triggered by something.

Sometimes, the smallest of things can trigger my pain to surface. At times, I feel like I'm being consumed by the pain. When this happens, I feel like nothing in my world feels okay. Not being okay contains all the things I don't like and all the things that feel wrong and stop me from being happy. This is what I want David to understand.

Dear Lisa

We both agree that I need to remain calm because that can't be helping my tummy issue. It's always been a reaction to my stress and so I'm trying really hard to remain calm and be present in the now, considering I'm okay now.

It can be difficult sometimes, like this morning, for example, when I woke up. I got flashbacks of things that have happened throughout my life. If I continue to think about it, it can send me down a path where I become upset, but I try not to allow that to happen, being always aware that there are unresolved issues and trauma that I have.

I'm hoping by writing this to you that I'll get more understanding of how to be there for myself, and to be able to see what I need.

My Three Marriages

29th May 2020

I have been married three times and divorced three times, too.

My first husband was Mark. My second husband, James. You met the first two, but you don't know about my third husband, Peter.

Mark

I met Mark when I was fifteen. We met at the Imperial War Museum in London when on a history trip with the school. Did you go on that trip, too?

Much of my life with Mark was happy. We were together for fifteen years, having spent the first four having a long distance relationship. Once I finished school, followed by three years at college, I moved

Dear Lisa

to London to live with him. We lived there for nine years.

Life was fairly simple back then. During those years we had our son, Tom, and when he was two years old, we decided to move back to Suffolk.

You know much of my life at that time, but what you don't know is what I'm still angry about.

I thought my relationship with Mark was very much about us. We seemed to work well as a team and I thought we trusted each other. We focused on each other with dedication and commitment.

What I didn't know was that he didn't think the same as me, and I didn't discover that until my marriage was ending with James. I only left Mark because he was very negative, whereas I am not.

Looking back, it was the best relationship I had, or so I thought. I look at all my relationships and don't actually know what they were. How many people are there that don't actually know the whole truth about their relationship and therefore are living a lie?

I'm still angry at Mark because of what he thought and what he told me. I was talking to him at the time that my marriage was ending with James. I can't remember what it was about, but it led him to tell me something that he'd kept to himself, even before Tom was born.

He told me that one day he came home from work and saw a man coming out of our flat. We lived on the end of a row of Victorian houses, and ours had been converted into two flats. These flats were owned by a housing association, and at times, men came round to service things.

My Three Marriages

As he was telling me this, about ten years after the event, I couldn't say who it was. He thought I was having an affair, but he hadn't said anything. I used to write a diary every single day and he told me that he'd looked in my diary for evidence. He didn't find any because there wasn't anybody else to write about. If he'd asked me on the day who it was, then I could have told him. What was he thinking? I never went anywhere without him, other than work.

I worked in a beauty salon where my colleagues were all women along with the clientele. I had no friends in London, where we lived. He was my life. He also knew I'd been abused. Can you imagine what a big thing it was to first have sex with him? He was my first, and everything about the physical side of our relationship was wonderful.

When we first made love, Mark didn't know about the abuse. I was seventeen years old and that first time was really scary. I was so worried that I wasn't a virgin and felt relieved when I saw the blood. It was a year later that I told Mark about the abuse I'd suffered, after my uncle died.

So, the reason Mark thought I was having an affair was because when he came home, I was in bed, apparently. I do know the year he was talking about because I had glandular fever. As usual, I tried to carry on as much as I could and still do, so I continued to go to work. I used to sleep at work during my lunch time and also on my days off, so that's probably why I was in bed.

Not long after that was when Mark and I went to Australia. My mum had recently died and whilst we were on the plane, I cried because I felt nearer to heaven and closer to her. Mark revealed to me that he thought I was crying because I'd left a man at home.

All of this makes me so angry. Every man I have ever been with, I have given my all to them. What upsets me the most is that this is what he thought of me. He thought I would do that, and he also thought that I *could* do that given my abuse. My whole life was with him. I can't believe he never asked me, at the time, about what he saw.

Apparently, he did tell his brother. I was blissfully carrying on as normal without a clue, but inwardly I knew because he was different towards me. I can remember the change when we were in Australia. I suppose he was less loving and that felt uneasy, but I didn't know why. I believe this was why our marriage ended.

I know you can't carry that belief about someone without it being destructive. I know this is not about me, but about Mark in some way. It's about a belief he has, but it's still hurtful.

What also hurts is I wanted to try for a baby when we returned home from Australia, but Mark was hesitant. I wonder if it was because of what he thought. I became pregnant with Tom straight away and that was the best choice I've ever made in my life. My son is an amazing person and I'm so proud of him.

James

As you know, after my first marriage ended, I married James.

When I was first married to him, I was very happy. There was something about him that reached my inner child, making me feel secure and loved. He was a gentle-man and very focused on my happiness, but this actually became his downfall. He didn't express what he wanted or didn't want. Instead, he tried to give me what he thought *I* wanted. That sounds good on the surface, but all it did was leave me feeling unwanted, and unfortunately, I felt that many times during the relationship.

That was when my inner child, **UNWANTED** surfaced. There were two main issues that caused **UNWANTED** to appear. The first was when James's children came to see him. His daughter was about ten years old when we first got together.

Obviously, it was a difficult time for the children with their parents splitting up. What I found difficult was the attention he gave to his daughter. I didn't mind her having attention of course, but it left me feeling neglected and pushed aside. I felt I lost my place in his life. It was painful to not receive attention whilst watching him give his undivided attention to someone else. This really upset me, and in those moments, I felt unwanted and neglected.

I also felt uncomfortable when his daughter sat next to him and he would stroke her leg. It was his way of showing affection, but from someone who has been abused it looked very inappropriate.

This attention that James gave his daughter affected me on quite a few different levels. It stems from when my parents got divorced and my step-mother arrived on the scene. My mum left my brother and me with my dad and his new wife and moved away to live with my uncle, the same one who abused me. The abuse happened when I visited them, and that was when I felt I'd lost both my parents and my place in their lives.

Dear Lisa

As much as the situation triggered the lost, neglected and unwanted parts of me, it also highlights the lack of safety and protection I had back then. Now, I am very protective over the welfare of children.

The second issue I had in my marriage to James, and the reason the marriage fell apart was due to a man I knew, who came to see me for a massage. He started giving me attention and was constantly flirting with me.

Now, at this point, I'd been struggling with the feelings of being pushed aside and losing my place, as I explained earlier, when James's daughter came to stay. The attention I was receiving had an effect on me and clearly the neglected part of me liked it. Having said that, I actually felt uneasy about it, too.

I told James about the attention and how it was making me feel and explained that I would never betray him. Unfortunately, his response was, "You can sleep with him if you want to." This isn't really what you want to hear from your husband. I'd have rather heard, *"I'm going to sort this out and tell him to leave you alone."* This meant that my inner children, **NEGLECTED** and **UNWANTED** now needed even more attention.

I see attention and the behaviours to get the attention as a way of being fed. It really is like food but for the mental and emotional bodies. That's why people overeat: comfort food. That's why so many addictions exist because it's all a way of getting fed. Unfortunately, though, it's actually like eating junk food, which is not very good for us.

I needed feeding and it was clear I was not going to be fed by my husband. Obviously, I got my food from the man who was giving me attention, and after I'd

My Three Marriages

slept with him and he left, I felt so upset. It was awful and really was like eating junk food. It's only more recently I've seen that what I needed was *loving* attention. I suppose my link to attention came from the unwanted sexual attention that I grew up with.

I was upset when James came home, and in his usual way he was very gentle with me. Having a gentle-man is lovely, but not in the absence of a protective one. Our marriage, from then on, wasn't just "us" anymore.

What I didn't understand at the time, was that I desperately needed to feel wanted, loved, looked after and protected, all the things I've had to learn to do for myself and still working on to strengthen those qualities.

This experience with James left me starving for more attention. You know I was able to, and I still *can* attract a lot of attention. I saw quite a lot of different men and some days more than just one. I remember, one day, I actually saw four different men. It seemed like a good thing then as I was receiving a regular supply of food. It doesn't seem a good thing now, though, because I don't eat that type of food anymore.

I feel like I've gone from one extreme to another, but actually, all I *have* done is learnt what is healthy for me. Now, I will only have what is good for me. Basically, I've addressed the balance, which is what all aspects of life and well-being need: to work in the realms of balance.

The rest of my marriage to James consisted of going to sex clubs. We actually kept it to just the two of us, but another time we tried having a foursome, which really upset me. I don't know how anyone en-

Dear Lisa

joys watching their partner with someone else. After that, we decided to have an open relationship, and what a mess that was. The more people I saw, the more in need of attention I became, because this was never going to give me what I needed. What I *did* need was love, not sex, but in the act of sex I felt wanted. I needed a loving, complete relationship with one man.

Finally, I became aware of what I was doing in seeing these men. I realised it wasn't me or what I wanted. It was at this point that James and I started living as friends, until he moved out when I met my third husband, Peter.

I told Peter about the open relationship I'd had and that it was not okay for me, and that what I really wanted was everything with one man.

Peter

We met when I agreed to be part of some activist protests with 'Fathers 4 Justice'. This took place in the North East of England, around Hartlepool. Peter lived not far from there and was also involved with Fathers 4 Justice.

He was helping to organise various protests that were planned. My role was to hand-cuff myself to the goal post during a football game at the Hartlepool stadium. I did that dressed as Cat Woman.

The funny thing was I'd never been to a football match before. I hand-cuffed myself around the goal post at half time, after finding the right moment to run on to the pitch. Once there, I thought, *"What do I do now?"* There was music playing so rather than just stand there, I thought I'd dance instead. The head-line in the papers the next day read, "Pole

My Three Marriages

Cat Dance". It's a real shame we have to protest and stand up to make things right, because why are they wrong in the first place?

After that event in Hartlepool, Peter kept in contact and we soon started seeing each other. Even in those early days we weren't a good match, but again I didn't walk away. I did end the relationship after about eighteen months, but then we got back together again.

Sometimes, I feel like I don't want to be on my own, which is strange as I'm self- sufficient. I feel it's because I want to be looked after. I want someone else to be there for me rather than just myself.

In the first few years of my marriage to Peter, he was quite insecure, always worrying about the male friends I had. I didn't actively see them, they just messaged me occasionally. I used to say to him, "All I want is you." I would walk along flying the flag for us: that's how I would describe it. I said to him, "It's a lovely feeling being yours, and being in this exclusive relationship means so much to me." However, whatever I said, he just didn't seem to see it.

One day, I was so fed up with trying to make him understand and stop him worrying, that I rang the man he worked for, who had actually been a witness at our wedding. I asked him to talk some sense into Peter. I was slightly annoyed when he asked if *I'd* actually done anything, to which I obviously said, "No." I mean, really? Anyway, he spoke to Peter, but it didn't make any difference.

When we met, I think, because we were in different places in our self-awareness, it caused a lot of tension between us. I think deep down he didn't feel good enough. We did go to a relationship workshop, though, and Peter said to me afterwards, "The lady that taught us said what you say." My response to him was, "What I say isn't just my way, but it's the balanced way which any coach would tell you." Going to this workshop really helped.

Over time, Peter evaluated himself, something I always admired him for, and eventually, we found ourselves in a really good place. We were kind to each other. We had a wonderful work-life balance. We loved nature and having days out. Life was good. Over this time, however, he would occasionally ask me, "What else would you like to do sexually?" I told him, "I'm happy with everything and I don't need to do anything differently."

For his fortieth birthday I had some photos taken of me for him. I purposely found a female photographer to take them. I wanted to be in nature with only my knickers on and a large red scarf, which I had with my wedding outfit. I wanted him to feel comfortable receiving the photos and I felt he would be happy knowing a lady took them.

Peter wouldn't be surprised seeing me naked in nature. We'd visited Scotland many times and I'd been naked with nearly every Scottish stone circle. Peter would take photos of me when we were there. I found it a very liberating experience and something quite magical whilst being one with the ancient stones. I still have a lovely photo of me at sunset, surrounded by beautifully coloured orbs, at the Ring of Brodgar on the Isle of Orkney.

Anyway, Peter loved the photos, but after that, he asked more about what else I'd like to do, sexually. Stupidly, I eventually told him, "I like a flowing massage, nothing sexual but more connected with lots of flowing strokes around my head, because that feels quite sensual to me." The beauty of having a massage like that, as a woman, is that if I became aroused, the practitioner wouldn't know. Instantly, Peter was urging me to book myself in for one.

This was the start of Peter giving me away. I can't believe it was nine years ago when it happened. My life since has been full of emotional pain and upset. I've learnt so much about myself, some of which I've already told you, and I'm just so glad I've managed to see the positives from what's happened and been able to strengthen myself.

Up until that point in my life, I'd already experienced enough abuse and unwanted sexual encounters. I really didn't want or need anymore. At this time, I didn't have my self-worth or self-respect and I was unable to keep myself safe. The neglected, unwanted parts of me started to surface, albeit subconsciously and discreetly at first. It was like those parts heard a little whisper which said, *"You aren't really wanted."* To prevent feeling the pain from that, once again those parts needed to receive attention, to feel loved and wanted.

I knew a male massage therapist very well, so I went to see him. I chose him because I knew him, and I suppose that made me feel safe. But it turned out to be very *un*safe. We actually had an intense connection. It was beautiful, not sexual, but incredibly loving. He spent time with me. He held me. He stroked me. He looked at me and I felt secure on the inside. I felt he was holding the neglected part of me.

I'm finding this quite emotional as I'm telling you. I'm not really sure why, maybe because it was so lovely. Maybe I'm upset because it all went wrong and now, he has nothing to do with me. Actually, he ended up being unkind, as did his new wife. Both of them are therapists, yet they never had compassion or the slightest thought of what things may have been like for me. His wife wasn't even around at the time, but he met her soon after. He obviously told her what happened, which wasn't easy for him, either. Where I'm compassionate towards him, they aren't towards me.

I approached him at a fair, where he was promoting his work. His wife, though still his girlfriend at that point, walked over and stood in front of me, then told me she didn't like me. She didn't even know me at the time, knew nothing about my life or what I'd experienced.

I found out recently that she's struggled in her life, which surprised me because I'd have thought she'd be more understanding and kinder to others, not less. It's clear she was feeling very insecure. However, it does make me angry when people who work in caring, spiritual professions don't act with empathy and compassion.

Even though I've been through so much, I always have compassion for others and I always see the good side of people. I don't see their bad behaviour as them being a horrible person. Instead, I see they must be hurting in some way for them to behave that way.

It's just not nice to be on the receiving end of someone being horrible to you. Maybe my upset now, as I tell you this, is because my pain is not being seen, and the part of me that hurts, needs love, not nastiness.

My Three Marriages

I mentioned earlier in this letter about the scar on my arm. It was during this time that I cut myself. I'd self-harmed before and mildly cut my leg, which has completely healed. My arm was much deeper though, and I'll have the scar forever. Now I'm upset again. I hate that I did that to myself, but it's also about the internal scars I hold. It's a very strange feeling of wanting to self-harm. I've thought about it a lot and feel I'm reaching out and saying, "Look, can you now see I'm in pain?" and "Please see my pain and be there for me. I need help."

The reason I cut my arm was because the loving connection I had with my massage friend caused Peter to feel insecure. He didn't want me to have a loving connection with anyone else; just a sexual one. We did try to have a threesome, but I think many men struggle joining a couple in that way, especially when there is a deep loving connection.

If it had just been sex, then that's different, but it wasn't like that for either of us. It obviously caused a lot of upset and difficulty for my friend, and let's face it, it's not an easy situation to cope with. I don't think any of us handled it very well and because of the connection, Peter wanted me to stop seeing my friend.

My internal reaction to Peter giving me away put me in emotional turmoil. I didn't want my friend to go because of the deep, loving, secure feeling I received from him. That was something I didn't want to lose.

I tried to make Peter see I wasn't going to leave him, and that all I wanted was to have this love and connection, but he wasn't having it. I was getting so upset and felt so helpless that I couldn't make him understand. I ran into the kitchen, grabbed a knife

Dear Lisa

and cut my arm. Unfortunately, I'd cut it so deeply, that Peter had to take me to the hospital.

It saddens me so much. I can't understand how anyone would want to allow someone else into their relationship in that way. The strength and beauty of being just the two of us, looking out for each other, was such a safe place to be. I wasn't safe at all and I wasn't capable of looking after myself.

NEGLECTED was fully present and dreadfully distraught. The love she was receiving was going away and she was left with someone who didn't really want her. Feeling such loss, I think subconsciously, I felt I needed to find someone who really *did* want me and so the unhealthy journey with Peter continued.

I'm feeling quite upset now so I'm going to get a cup of tea and maybe some dark chocolate...

...That's better; I'm feeling more settled now.

The unhealthy journey with Peter lasted for about eighteen months. Everything I've told you so far has been so easy to write. Now, I feel like I'm stuck in mud and I've lost my sense of flow.

I want to tell you everything, but I'm scared because I feel bad about it. This made me realise that if I'm not honest, I'm not being there for myself.

I need to show my inner child, **BAD,** that she is *not* bad and she has not been looked after or protected. By me not telling you as it was, I'm hiding **BAD** away, like I'm ashamed of her. But that just confirms to her, even more, that she *is* bad.

Ultimately, everything lies within me. The most important thing is what I think of myself and not what others think of me. I need to give my inner children a voice. They need to be heard, listened to and

My Three Marriages

understood so they can receive the love and attention they need.

There's still so much I don't understand about what Peter wanted to do. I understand myself and how I went along with it, but I don't understand how he could share me and want to watch me with other men. I've asked him, but he says he doesn't know why. I have my own theory, though. I'm more self-confident with who I am and I believe that caused him to feel not good enough. He clearly has a belief of not being wanted, so to sabotage his marriage, he gave his loving, committed wife away. That's how it seems to me.

I watched a programme the other day on the television about swingers. I didn't really want to see it, but I needed to see why people were doing this. It seems my thoughts around it were correct.

Everyone I saw actually had a confidence issue or didn't feel good about themselves in some way. It was clear that they just didn't know how to make themselves feel better. Instead, they were feeding on sex, using it as their junk food, which of course only ever temporarily made them feel better.

I could relate, in some ways, because I've used sex to get the attention I needed, but it never fixed anything within me. Actually, it caused more damage. At the time, I thought it was great, but now I cringe when I think of it.

Of course, I cringe because **BAD** shows up and clearly still needs a lot more loving attention from me. Basically, I feel bad at the things I did. I know I need to remind myself that I was only trying to survive and get what I thought I needed. I didn't have my eyes open to see it differently then, like I do now, and I can feel good knowing that I can now look after myself. I can keep myself safe and only allow loving attention when people are genuinely caring and respecting me.

When I was with Peter, I couldn't keep myself safe. So, I allowed myself to continue being given away by him because of the attention I needed. I wasn't feeling loved and wanted and this momentarily made me feel better. It's interesting though, as most of what happened and what I allowed to happen was in an environment which was more loving. I rejected the more extreme things that Peter wanted to do, like taking me to a sex cinema, where he told me a man had taken his wife to have sex with thirty different men, in one evening. Deep down, I think I knew I needed love and was never going to allow that to happen.

Peace comes when you make peace with yourself. I realise that more by writing about what has happened to me, because of the feelings that arise. I realise I've judged myself and not given myself enough understanding, but at that time, I wasn't capable of doing it any differently.

I suppose I should be proud of myself now with where I am today, with how much I've learnt and how much I can now look after myself. In fact, the more I'm there for all my inner children, the stronger and wholesome I feel. It's a journey of discovery; not an overnight fix. Actually, it's not even a fix because I'm not broken and don't need mending. I just need love. Now, I know how to love myself so much more.

I've just had a thought that I'm still not really telling you much about what went on with Peter. I want

My Three Marriages

to tell you about my childhood abuse also and so I will tell you then, because basically, it *was* abuse.

Peter knew I only ever wanted him and I told him how important that was to me when I first met him. He knew I hadn't been happy having an open relationship when I was with James. He didn't keep me safe and it wasn't what I'd asked for. He disregarded what I'd told him and I felt like I'd been abused all over again.

I had been abused as a child and then, in adulthood, I'd given myself away when I didn't feel wanted by James. I knew this wasn't good for me and I stopped it because I only ever wanted to be with that one special person. I needed that person to love and want me for themselves. Never did I want them to bring me more emotional harm and abuse. I couldn't protect myself, but Peter knew what I needed.

Abusers prey on the weak, helpless children who cannot protect themselves, and children trust the adults. I felt just the same with Peter. He was my husband and I trusted him to look after me. At least now, if I'm not looked after, I can look after myself. I should, however, be able to trust people, because abusing an innocent vulnerable person is simply not, and never will be acceptable.

Dear Lisa

The Abuse

1ˢᵗ June 2020

I don't remember telling you that I was abused, but I'm sure I must have mentioned it. Now, I understand so much more about it and the affect it has had on me. I want to tell you in detail because I know it will help some more of my inner children to surface. The more they surface, the more I can bring love to them and to myself.

My abuse started when I was six years old and ended at aged thirteen. My mum left my dad to be with his brother, my uncle. She also left me and my brother behind, although my dad did fight to keep us. I'm so pleased he did because the abuse happened whenever I visited my mum.

I can't remember the first time my uncle did something to me, though I do remember it starting in the first house him and my mum were living in, which was in or near Bury St Edmunds. It's strange not to have a memory of the first time because I also can't remember how that felt. My most vivid memory at

The Abuse

this house was one night when I was asleep. I woke up to find my uncle opening my legs. I remember feeling uncomfortable and pretending to stay asleep, then I rolled over and he went away. My mum was in the same room, asleep, as I slept in a bed in their room. It's the only vivid memory I have there. After that house, they then moved to Wretton, to live and work on a chicken farm. It was there that I remember the abuse well.

I don't think my brother and I visited my mum regularly, like many children do, as in every other weekend. Every time we went, though, something happened. Now, I wonder what my uncle was thinking. Why, and how, he managed to do this to me. I know I was a sensitive child; I'm a sensitive person and I would have been quite vulnerable.

It's so sad to think that as an innocent child, open to love, wanting to *be* loved, that I wasn't looked after and nurtured. Instead, I was manipulated in a subtle way. The worse part of it all is that I felt very much a part of what was happening and this is where the feeling of being bad comes from.

As a child, I didn't see the manipulation and can't even remember it today. Instead, I see what he did to me and that I allowed it to happen. I know now that it wasn't my fault, but it is really hard to come to terms with knowing I let it happen. I was, however, under thirteen years old and powerless to stop it, or even understand any of it. All I knew was I was receiving pleasure and being a part of this secret, which caused me to feel guilty, ashamed and bad.

My uncle was obviously careful not to do anything when my mum was around. Although, looking back, she must have been around, but maybe she thought everything was innocent. I suppose he just found the opportunities where she didn't see anything.

I remember she would go to bed early and my brother and I would stay up watching the television with my uncle. I would lie next to my uncle on the sofa and he would play with me between my legs. He did that a lot. I loved having my feet tickled and he would start off doing that, but then his hand would travel up my leg. I'd get into bed with him in the mornings and this is what I find so difficult to comprehend, because *I* went into *his* room. I don't understand where my mum was at that point, but surely, she couldn't have thought me being in bed with my uncle was appropriate?

Everything he did to me was pleasurable. Basically, he was giving me an orgasm, either with his fingers or by rubbing his penis against me, and of course, orgasms felt nice. I suppose I felt loved and that I was receiving attention. He would also take me over to the chicken sheds and touch me there. I remember one time, in the office, him bending me over trying to get his penis inside of me, which he didn't achieve as I was too small.

As I got older and became more aware, I started to feel more uncomfortable around him. When I got my period, I told him because I was worried. His response was, "You be nice to me and I'll be nice to you." I was young and didn't understand the extent of what he was actually doing. That's why, when I first had sex with Mark, I was so worried I wasn't a virgin.

I told Mark about the abuse, soon after my uncle had died. I was eighteen. A tree fell on his car while he was driving and it killed him outright. His death

The Abuse

allowed me to have a voice. That was thirty-four years ago and at that time abuse wasn't really talked about or understood like it is today. Also, while he was alive, I felt powerless. I didn't actually want to tell anyone then anyway because I felt so bad and thought I'd done something very wrong.

I've read other stories about people being abused with the emphasis on them being a victim, which, of course they were. But what I've never heard is anyone saying how it was pleasurable. I said this to a lady at the Sue Lambert group. She said to me, "This is the first time I have ever heard anyone say that and I can relate to it." There must be many abused people afraid to say they felt pleasure and probably feel so much worse because they think they should have hated it.

I obviously hated the fact I was being abused. It took away my innocence. I was used and abused, but I know all too well the awful feelings from receiving that pleasure: the guilt, the shame, and the intense feelings I had of allowing those things to happen. As a child, I couldn't see I'd been manipulated to a place where he could do that to me. These are the feelings I had all over again with Peter, but even worse, because I was an adult then, still living like the abused child who was allowing these things to happen.

I learnt, from a counsellor, about how abused people can desensitise themselves to be able to cope with what is happening. Peter took this as confidence. Actually, when I was desensitised, I could do many things. I felt like I had a protective shell around me and I was inside that shell. Anything happening outside of that I couldn't feel. The problem with that, however, was after the event. Once the shell was gone, I saw and felt the reality of what happened. Then, I felt shame and disgust all over again.

Now, I'm more aware of when I desensitise myself. Lisa, it has been such a difficult process of learning to speak up and be able to say to people if I don't like something. It is still something I'm working on. It's just the small things now though, where I don't instantly react, but tend to shut down instead. I *can* react if someone tries to kiss me, who shouldn't be. If someone gives me a hug and their hands start to wander, I tend to desensitise at first, but then I will move away. I'd love to just move away and say, "Don't do that." Even with all the manipulation I've had, I still seem to trust people. I believe they will be respectful and treat me right, but it seems so many are more interested in what *they* want.

One of the worst things about being abused is how it takes away self-worth, self-respect and the inability for self-protection. There should be a programme available to anyone who has been abused, to help them become aware of the effects of abuse and teach how to respect, protect and value themselves. With the lack of self-respect and the desensitisation, I wasn't capable of keeping myself safe. That caused me to do things that just disrespected me further.

I never looked for these sexual experiences; Peter did that. But I did allow some things to happen. Actually, Peter said to me, "I want you to have one hundred cocks." I didn't agree to things. I just listened, shocked inside, knowing I was being treated as an object. The thought of my husband seeking and allowing men to use me, hurts me so much. I'm not an object to be used. I'm a wonderful, loving, caring lady to be cherished, protected and looked after.

The Abuse

There were two occasions where we'd booked a massage. At the end of both, Peter said to the therapist, "You *can* have her." As I write this, I think, *"How dare he?"* I wasn't his property. I'm upset writing this now, and I'm upset I was treated this way and couldn't look after myself. One of these therapists actually declined, thankfully. Looking back, it was so much like my childhood abuse. I was receiving stroking, pleasurable attention through massage, but then being violated.

Another time when I was upset about something, Peter and I went out for a walk to cheer me up. We went to the forest and were followed by a group of men. This area was obviously a part of the forest where men look for sexual encounters. It's near a dogging area, but this was during the day. It was one occasion where Peter thought I was confident, but I was just desensitised. We started kissing, which encouraged the men to follow us into the trees and join us. My breasts were out and Peter said, "Hasn't she got lovely breasts?" Peter had his penis out. I bent over to give him a blow job while a man took me from behind. Now I cringe every time I drive past this area. I remember after all of the experiences, feeling quiet inside, like a little girl hiding away: lonely.

Wherever Peter and I went, I felt he was looking for a man to join us. We had some hotel experiences, one with a massage therapist and one with a younger man, who was just looking for sex. A lot of the massage encounters weren't actually unpleasant, but they were horrible, if you understand what I mean? They were physically pleasurable, but emotionally destroying.

Dear Lisa

We saw a tantric massage therapist several times and had sex. There was nothing wrong with the experience, but it just wasn't something that was good for me. All of this wasn't what I wanted to do. Lots of people have a tantric massage, go to sex clubs and engage in similar activities. They all bring physical pleasure, but all these things just make me feel like an object. There is no pleasure happening inside of me with my feelings.

It's going to take me some time to stop feeling bad about what I allowed to happen. A friend said to me recently, "It doesn't matter how many sexual partners you've had because that is in the past. All of the experiences of life have brought you to this point." That helped me feel a little better about what I allowed to happen. I suppose most of us can look back and feel bad about some things we've done, but when I think of that and then think about me now, the person that I am, I do actually feel very good about myself.

I'd been abused and I'd allowed myself to be abused all over again. You know, Lisa, the abuse is one thing, but much worse is the damage it caused and the mess it has caused me to make later in my life. Going through all of this has at least shown me what was missing with my lack of self-respect, self-worth and self-protection, but it's been an incredible way to learn.

The last person to have a threesome with Peter and myself was David. I feel he rescued me from what was happening, because he fell in love with me. He wanted me and very quickly, didn't want Peter to have me. David would never share me.

The Abuse

Peter found David on a website where people are looking for sex. He messaged David, pretending to be me and I still remember the first time we met him. It was in a Costa coffee shop, in April 2013. David was quite nervous, as he wasn't very confident then. I'm obviously used to seeing people with my job and because of my open, kind, and friendly nature, people do soon feel at ease with me.

I'm glad David came into my life. The last seven years have been very challenging, but I will always be grateful that he rescued me from the situation with Peter.

David

2nd June 2020

After meeting David that first time, Peter and I arranged to meet him again, and a few weeks later, he came to visit us at our home. What I most remember about this day was what David noticed about the way Peter and I were with each other. I remember making some lunch with Peter helping as though we were a team. We were being kind to each other, because that's how we were together. I learnt after that it hadn't been like that for David in his marriage. After lunch, we had a bath together and all went to bed. We had sex, which was very gentle and caring, making it feel like a pleasant experience.

David started to spend more time with us, joining us on days out occasionally. It didn't take long, though, probably just a few months, before tensions started to form. David developed feelings for me and wanted more. He wanted to just be with me. Peter started to stress again which meant the time I was having with him wasn't enjoyable anymore. He be-

David

came more and more stressed and David became more and more demanding. I was stuck in the middle, trying to manage both of them. This carried on until December 2013 when Peter and I split up and he moved out.

Peter has never gone away and I think he will always be there looking out for me in some way. For much of the last seven years, both him and David have been in my life. My neglected child liked having them both there, as did my alone child. I needed something from them both, but I never felt happy for long. Most of the time, the situation just brought a lot of stress for us all. Basically, we just kept feeding each other junk food, rather than actually being there for ourselves. Feeding ourselves with good wholesome food would have made us feel great. Instead, not meeting our own needs caused us to remain needy of each other.

There have been many times when I've missed my life with Peter. We had a good life together, but I struggled to go back to him because he gave me away. In all this time, he hasn't been able to make me feel wanted.

When Peter and I split up, David left his wife. He rented a cottage, not far from me, for six months. At this time, David's children were very young and he also had some debt. My life back then, as it is now, was very simple. I'd kept things in order and stayed in control of my finances. It was seven years ago and my son had already left home.

I remember the first Christmas when David saw his children. They visited on Boxing Day, just for the day. When he took them home, I stayed at the cottage to tidy up. I stood at the kitchen sink, washing up, crying and feeling like I'd landed in somebody else's life. I have had that feeling over and over again throughout the last seven years, every time I'm in the relationship with David. I felt like I wasn't living my life the way I wanted to live it. It's a horrible and very upsetting feeling.

I've written many journals over the years I've been seeing David, particularly from 5th July 2013 to 23rd August 2014. I'd known David for only three months in that July, and this is what I wrote:

"Heaven, Hell or Healing?

5th July 2013. I can't decide if my life is like being in heaven or hell. Sometimes, I feel like I'm in heaven but soon after I feel like I'm in hell. Over the last eighteen months I have experienced huge extremes of heaven and hell.

I've entered into a journey. I could get off now, at any time, but I don't. Why? Maybe what I'm experiencing on this journey will eventually lead me to healing. I wonder if it ever exists at the deeper levels, with huge traumas and events that have been carried around in the depths of a being. Always there, lurking in the depths, until a situation causes it to surface. Do we avoid those situations and only allow ourselves to be in the environment where we feel at peace, or do we allow the wounds to open, in some chance to heal?

It seems of recent years, I choose to stay in the situation which causes me to face my past in the hope for healing, but I know there will be a limit to what I will cope with. The thing is the heaven between the hell keeps this journey bearable.

David

What do I find most difficult? What I find difficult is dealing with all the people around me and all the emotions which come from fear, causing unbalanced behaviour and pressures.

What do I want? I can't deny having two men in my life brings heavenly experiences, but it's not easy. I want one man who I can love, adore, admire and give my all to. I want us to be so special to each other, to have a sacred, honest, and trustworthy relationship.

Yes, I can love two men. We all can love many but love each person in a different way. Each connection is different, the learning is different, but there is a different level of commitment to the one life partner.

How do I feel? How do you love two people in that way, loving them for different reasons, being torn emotionally between the two, trying to keep both happy? The getting it wrong is so draining, putting my feelings aside, allowing myself to have less to keep one of them happy. Someone always seems to be unhappy.

This stopped and then it started again, why? Can I live without this? I know, in a new relationship, I would not want this. I want to be worshipped and loved by one person and to love and worship one person in return.

I find myself in this very strange situation. I have no idea what it means. I don't know where I'm viewing it all from, be it my emotions, my inner child or my mind. I feel like I'm waiting for clarity to be revealed. I can't make any decisions because I don't want to make them from the wrong place.

I think I feel there needs to be change because the situation is rarely smooth. There is always upset and tension. Maybe I could do this if it ran easily and smoothly, where everyone is happy, secure and at ease. I think our emotions don't allow for such situations and that's why two people together is so much easier, but I have to have David. He gives my inner child all the love I never received. My inner child wants and needs David. But I do know Peter is there for me, will always love me and be loyal to me.

2nd August 2013. My confusion causes me to look at so many things: the past with Peter, the length and difficulties of our relationship, the hard work, teaching him, lack of attention in the way I needed it, this process of sharing me over the last eighteen months, the lack of protection and behaviour towards me.

Look at what I would lose, the lifestyle and the position we have got to in our lives together.

I had a conversation with David about being okay and I don't think that I've ever really been okay. I really believe nobody truly loves me and I hate that along with the feeling it gives me.

I feel all that I have been through I cannot heal because it's too traumatic. The answer is to stay in healthy, loving, supportive environments and not situations which are anything to do with what I've suffered or how I have been treated.

I actually feel so unloved by all the significant adults in my life throughout my childhood and now by my husbands. I just don't seem to have put myself in healthy relationships, for example, one didn't trust me, one gave me away and one devalued me and didn't keep me to himself. Why is it going to be different with anyone else?

*3rd **August 2013**. I'm feeling very empty and emotional today. Something feels different since I was upset a few evenings ago when David wouldn't make love to me. I understand why because of the tension that is there. I know he loves me and wants me in that way, but I felt hurt and rejected. I now feel like I can't get enough of him, to make the empty feelings go away.*

*10th **August 2013**. Bad dream last night, away in Edinburgh at the moment. I dreamt David was seeing someone else, as well as me. I found out and was upset he'd lied to me, so I ended it with him. He was upset as I said I was going to choose him. I think I had this dream because I'm finding it difficult to feel anything with Peter and I'm worried David is going to have sex with his wife. I suppose I hope he can't do it, because then it would show me how much he wants me.*

*18th **August 2013**. It's been a stressful week. David did have sex with his wife. I understand why. He thought I wouldn't ever agree to be with him. I always find it difficult that he's scared of being alone and therefore keeps his safety net firmly in place.*

Last weekend with Peter was different. I couldn't be intimate with him. I feel this week has been quite damaging with David. I still feel love the same, but I also feel disappointed.

*19th **August 2013**. Been thinking about David today and him focusing on his safety net with his wife. I want him to show me he's prepared to risk everything for me and let go of things he no longer needs. I don't want him to do things because I want* *him to, but because he wants to. I want him to come to me and say, "Look at what I've done because I want you so much." How could anyone refuse that, especially with the love we have? But instead, he's given his focus to his existing life. I feel he needed to show me that because it was him who asked me to spend my life with him. He asked me to be with him.*

21st September 2013. *Today is* **Peace One Day**. *I haven't seen David since Monday. We decided not to see each other because he can't cope with seeing me and then not seeing me and I'm trying to see if I can reconnect to Peter, to get the intimate side of our relationship back.*

Since Monday, I've been upset every day. I feel lifeless without David, yet I know Peter loves me and I love him and the life we have. I can cope with Peter holding me, but it feels so wrong when it is sexual. I just think of how it is with David, how it feels to be with him in that way.

I realise, in my life, what makes me happy is how much love I receive in the way I'm treated. The way I'm touched, looked at and held. The romance, being thought of, being with someone who can't get enough of me and shows me in the way of a fairytale romance.

29th September 2013. *I told David last night that I'm going to make this situation normal. Peter shouldn't have wanted this. I should have said "No" as all this is wrong. The situation with David is wrong. I'm hurting by all of the mess this situation brings and all that David needs to sort out.*

Now I need to see if I can be happy with Peter. I felt relieved at first, but now I'm so upset and I've gone back to feeling lifeless again. There's some-

thing about the way David loves me. He seems so focused on me, like I'm the most precious thing in the universe. He tells me that and I feel it by the way he touches me, holds me and needs me.

3rd October 2013. *I'm sitting by the conservation pond at Kelling Heath; I love it here. I'm on my own today, just me and my thoughts. It's peaceful and calm. I like being on my own because there's no stress or hassle to deal with. It's tiring keeping two people happy. Just as things seem relaxed, one or both have a wobble. I know the situation isn't easy, but it started in an unconventional way and it's hard to stop because of the love involved. I want to have David's love, and I know I'd maybe get over him with support in time, but the way he loves me will stay with me forever.*

My life with Peter, as a whole, is good, but to get everything I want, I will have to ask. Peter is easily distracted, so his focus is lost and I feel we miss out on beautiful, loving moments which make me feel loved, special and wanted. I want Peter to be happy with me, to enjoy our time, instead of stressing, which is causing problems between us. Spending time with him isn't enjoyable anymore.

David isn't going to leave his wife on his own accord which I have a problem with. I think he needs to build a foundation to enable him to be in a better position to start a new relationship. For now, I just want to be detached from his personal life and enjoy amazing loving times with him, just us, loving each other. I love having him love me. I only hope Peter can cope with the time I spend with David and I hope David is satisfied with the amount of time he has with me.

Dear Lisa

I do worry slightly about Peter and why he wanted to do this in the first place. There is clearly something about him that's excited about what is perceived as wrong to do. Fantasy is okay, but making it real is dangerous, as he found out.

I do question whether being on my own is what I should do now, but I think with a little more time, I will know.

23rd August 2014. *I did a healing exercise with a friend today. He asked me what things are important to me in a relationship and why.*

I wrote down love, commitment, honesty, equality, happiness and security.

Why?

Love = Lack of love, needing love and attention.

Commitment = giving 100 percent and prioritising each other.

Honesty = knowing the other person won't hurt you, and freedom.

Equality = looking after each other.

Happiness = fun and positive times.

Security = makes me feel safe.

Love and honesty I have stated in a negative way so I needed to turn them into being positive.

Love: I recognise abundance of love from everyone. I deserve the best. I respect myself. I delight in all my good qualities. I feel the love from knowing the loving, caring, happy, kind, open-hearted, successful and beautiful person that I am. I have freedom to make better choices.

David

Honesty: I deserve to live in freedom with truth and reality, to enjoy my values and morals.

Love has held me back because of the need that I have. Therefore, I have accepted much that is not right for me and invested so much into another to make it right, and I settled for less.

Feeling the love for myself and who I am helps me make better choices. I can be more choosey and have someone who enhances my life, as well as me enhancing theirs.

I want to spend time being me, enjoying the things I like to do and spending time with different people who I enjoy seeing; to indulge in myself and my own life for a while, building up and really connecting to my values and being able to live that way in freedom.

So, at the moment, I want to spend time with people, do things for each other, but without sexual intimacy. I'd like this to include David. I may be disappointed by what he does next but being choosey and allowing myself to have what's right for me, will help me with any disappointment, because David, as he stands today, is not what I choose.

My need for love has meant I haven't chosen wisely. I hope now I can change that pattern and make better choices. No more putting up with what I don't like because they love me.

I'm reminding myself about living in the present and not to look back at how things were, but what they have become and how I feel about them now. What is in my life now? Am I repeating patterns which don't serve me? Am I doing it better and not worrying about the future? Because in the NOW I am doing okay."

So, Lisa, this was the turmoil of the first seventeen months of knowing David. Little did I know I would keep repeating the same old pattern over and over again *and* for another six years. The problem was, I could see what I was doing, but I didn't know how to stop it. I knew the mistakes I was making and *had* made, and I could even see what I needed to do, but I could never do it for long. The missing part was the lack of understanding of how much my inner child needed, how desperate for love she was. My failure was not seeing it was *me* that she most needed.

You can see with what I've written in my journal that I was looking outside of myself to give my inner child what she needed. Looking back, I see my confusion then and can now see clearly why I couldn't leave. I thought David could give me what I needed and at times he did, but that's not healing. I was handing the power over to him, which gave him the ability to control me and play with my emotions. It rendered me weak.

I wrote that maybe I could never have healing because of the trauma. Now I know that healing comes from within me and understanding and building a relationship with my inner children is giving me the healing I need. Not as a fix to make me better, but as inner strength and inner love. I'm constantly being there for myself, listening to how I need to meet my needs for the rest of my life.

I now know too, that any future relationships will be different because *I* am different. I will protect myself and only allow myself to be in a relationship that is good for me. I will only stay in and choose healthy environments, because this is where I should place myself. When I'm there for me, I have the strength to remove myself from what isn't working for me.

It was in 2015 when I started understanding and listening to my inner children. It's taken another five years to fully understand how to be there for myself. I've gathered much information and skills along the way, although, I wish I'd learnt this years ago, so I could have stopped repeating the cycle for so long. I'm so glad I know, because now and in the future, things will be different.

At the beginning of 2015 I was feeling emotional and upset much of the time. So, I decided I needed to do more things to help myself. I attended a couple of courses which I could use in my work, but also for myself. One course I attended was 'Laughter Yoga'. Do you remember how easily I laugh and the sound of it? It's so funny. My sister has the same laugh, so can you imagine what it's like when we're together? Laughter Yoga was great and I found it really uplifting to do. I did a little video during lockdown and posted it on Facebook. It looks like I'm a crazy woman, but it made me laugh.

In June 2015, I attended a weekend workshop in London, run by a man called Jeff Foster. I came across this man on Facebook and his posts really caught my attention. I felt that finally I'd found someone who is being real. What I love the most about what he says, are his words surrounding inner children and allowing the pain to be present. His way is so refreshing and so different, and in my view, it makes perfect sense. I've written in my notes from that weekend that we are vast beings, capable of holding everything. Everything wants to be let in,

Dear Lisa

held, to have a home, and it holds great intelligence which will teach you.

It's still taken me another five years to get to this point, but practice makes perfect. The more I do things, the better I become. I can see how, over this time, I now understand how to meet my pain, and listen to and meet my own needs.

Protecting Children

8th June 2020

I've spent years training and working with touch and I know what touch can do. I also know, because of being abused, that I'm very conscious of touch and it being appropriate. I'm also aware that my ways may be a bit more reserved when it comes to touching children. A massive part of that is about keeping them safe and teaching them what is safe touch.

When I met David, he allowed his daughter to kiss him on the lips, as did other members of her family. She saw us kissing and she wanted to do it more, not just a peck. She was very young at the time and her mum said she'd been doing that more with her. I never kissed my son on the lips and I don't think that's acceptable. I know other families do, but personally, I think it leaves them open to be taken advantage of.

Children are so genuinely loving and enjoy lapping up attention, but they need to be kept safe and taught what is acceptable. I looked at David's daughter and saw this sweet, loving, innocent girl. She was open to love and affection and I saw she could so easily be taken advantage of. She reminded me of myself. That was me, when I was young, and I *was* taken advantage of with no power to stop it.

My nephew kisses my sister on the lips and recently, when he wanted to kiss me, I offered him my cheek. He then asked, "Why can't I kiss you on the lips?" My sister and I explained, "Some people don't do that." I think I added that my lips were just for David.

I understand everyone's different in how they do things, but for me, I worry about children and their safety. Years ago, abuse wasn't talked about as it is now. The awareness of it going on, and that so much of it was going on, just wasn't there. Hopefully now however, children are more aware and that will give them more protection. Unfortunately, abusers are very good at manipulating and abuse doesn't just happen all at once. It's often a very slow and subtle process, which actually makes a child feel loved, wanted and special. It's basically what's known as the grooming process. This can happen with an adult, so what hope has an innocent child got?

Protecting children is vital to me and I get very, very angry if they are not looked after. People say they would give their life for their child. I have actually had this feeling. One day, Peter, my husband, was arguing with my son and it sounded particularly

Protecting Children

aggressive. I was upstairs at the time and ran down to the room in which they were arguing, then stood between them in order to protect my son. I can't remember what I said to Peter, but nobody hurts my child. I didn't care what could have happened to me as long as my son was safe.

You probably remember when I was with James, that we were both a very active part of 'Fathers for Justice'. We joined because after about two years of us being together, he lost all contact with his children. Even to this day he has no contact with them and doesn't even know where they are. This should never happen. A child should not lose a parent in this way and more importantly, the law should not allow it.

The heart-breaking stories of children who don't have a loving father anymore, are just tragic. Those children are missing out on a relationship not only with their father, but with their paternal family also. How can this be allowed to happen? It's simply not acceptable and no child should lose a loving parent from their lives.

The environment that children grow up in is so important to how they become in their adult life. A wise parent will separate their own fears, insecurities and desires from them having an effect on their child. When parents end their relationship, it doesn't need to affect the child, though it will affect them in some way, of course, but it doesn't need to be made worse for them by the parents involving the children into the mess they have created as adults.

Children are often misunderstood because they are not capable of expressing what they feel. Instead, they show what they feel by the way they behave, which is no different to what we do as adults; the hurt inner child is still expressing itself by its behaviour.

Children aren't capable of so many things because they are children and therefore still have skills to learn. It's the job of the parent to teach them, but far too often the parent lacks understanding and only sees the behaviour, instead of seeing what the child is trying to express. So, whenever a child is unhappy, their behaviour needs to be seen as a way of expressing they're not okay for some reason. Being seen and supported creates safety for a child. It's what we, as adults, are doing with our inner children: showing them we are there.

I think there's a big part of me that feels I have to get things right and that's why I feel others should be getting them right, too. I need to realise nobody is perfect, and neither am I. More importantly, it's okay to get it wrong. I can't be expected to get it right all the time and I shouldn't expect others to, either. I think I really struggle with this, because I'm angry that the adults didn't look after me when I was young. So, my inner child, **ANGRY**, surfaces when people appear not to be doing the right thing, especially if children are being mistreated.

Underneath the anger is pain. It's painful not to be looked after. I have that pain and I don't want it to be created in someone else. I think that I'm so aware of the painful, hurtful emotions I have, I see I'm missing some of their playmates. I need to spend time to find them so they can help. Maybe I just need to listen more. I can't help if I don't know what they need. I've always said, "80% of healing comes from being aware, because if you can't see it, you can't do anything about it." So, the hard bit is recognising what's present, then you only have 20% of the work to do after that.

Reflecting on the time when James's daughter came to visit, I was struggling with the situation and my feelings. I was unaware that what I felt was actually highlighting what had happened to me as a child and that the memories of those events were triggering that. With the loss of contact James had with his children, the situation disappeared and so did my painful feelings. This obviously made me feel better, but didn't actually give me the help I needed, and still do.

I first went to get help in my early twenties, thirty years ago. I was referred to the hospital to see a psychiatrist and he told me basically that I was okay. Like I said, on the surface, I'm very strong and together, but how can anyone truly be okay when they've been sexually abused? If I felt okay, I wouldn't have been asking for help.

Thirty years on, I don't think it's much better. Yes, there is much more awareness but it's still hard to get help. That's why the Sue Lambert Trust, and organisations like that, are so vital, because they offer the help that is needed.

What I'd like to see is a programme for people that have been abused. Can you imagine if the professionals had a programme that I could have attended to explain the effects of abuse to me when I was twenty years old? It could have taught me about self-respect, self-worth, how to look after myself, protect myself and make healthy choices. It could have also taught me the way abusers work, how they manipulate and that none of it was my fault. If only

I'd been taught these things back then, they would have saved me from giving myself away in my adult life. It would have stopped me from letting people manipulate and take advantage of me.

As far as I'm aware, there isn't anything like this available. Surely, there must be enough knowledge about abuse now for a group of professionals to put such a programme together? *"Prevention is better than cure,"* and with such a programme, so much could have been prevented in my life. I didn't get the help I needed and that caused me to endure more abuse in my life simply because I didn't have the skills to prevent it. I had my self-respect and the ability to say no stripped away from me. People can be helped and the damage caused by abuse can be dramatically reduced by having such a programme. I think this is something that definitely needs looking into.

Breast Cancer

9th June 2020

2016: I remember it very well. I started the year being single, having left the relationship with David, once again, after the Christmas period.

Peter and David were still in my life, both of them, I suppose, still wanting to be with me and both still thinking about themselves.

Peter lied to me and I discovered that David was back on an internet site showing pictures of his cock whilst looking for sex. I was going through breast cancer treatment at the time. That was a hell of an emotional journey, not just the cancer, but also from the emotional hurt from the people around me. I did, however, learn about those who really did care about me, and they made that year so much more bearable.

Dear Lisa

My journey began in the February. I was in the bath one evening and I thought the outside of my left breast felt different to my right. David was with me at my house at the time. We weren't an item then, but in the usual pattern, we kept contact and started spending more time together. I asked him to see if he could feel any difference with my left breast. He could, but it didn't feel like a lump. I rang the doctor the next day and got an emergency appointment, to which David accompanied me. The doctor referred me to the hospital.

Both Peter and David took me to my various hospital appointments, both of them there with me, offering much-needed support.

It was in that February that someone told me they'd seen David on a website with pictures of his cock on show. I confronted him and he denied it, but I knew too much detail about it, and after telling him, he eventually admitted it was true. I was really upset. I know he did it because he believed he couldn't find another partner in any other way, but after how we'd met, all I'd gone through and how horrible and wrong it had all felt, knowing that he felt that too, made me feel hurt and disappointed that he'd done it. He never actually met anyone, probably because I found out very quickly, and deep down, he didn't really want that. He did it because I'd gone again and somehow, he needed to survive. It was the food he chose to feed himself, which ended up leaving a nasty taste in his mouth.

At my first hospital appointment, I saw the consultant and as she could feel something she referred me for a mammogram and ultrasound. This was the first mammogram I'd had, as I was only forty-seven. Both

Breast Cancer

the mammogram and the ultrasound showed nothing, and I was told to go back in five weeks when, if it still felt the same, I would have a biopsy. I did go back five weeks later and had the biopsy, which alarmingly showed cancerous cells. Peter took me to the appointment and he was there when I received this news. We were both naturally upset. I then had to have another appointment for an MRI scan.

It was during this time of being diagnosed that Peter lied to me. I was at his house one day, when he had to pop out for a short while. He left me with his iPad. Shortly before he'd gone out, I'd asked him, "How do the different people fit into your life and what level of contact do you have with your ex-girlfriend?" I don't know why I did it, but something just popped into my head, when using his iPad, to click on his messages. This is where I discovered he had lied to me.

The messages with his ex-girlfriend were different to what he'd told me. He'd led me to believe that they just said, "Hi" to each other occasionally, but in these messages, they were arranging to meet. They were also a lot friendlier than he had implied.

I wasn't in a relationship with Peter, so he could do whatever he wanted, but lying about it was not acceptable, because he wasn't being honest. When he returned, I was upset and told him to take me home. He told me he lied because he didn't want me to go away, but unfortunately for him, it had the opposite effect. I would much rather be told the truth so I can make my choices on what's real.

Whether it's Peter or anyone else, I don't expect their life to be perfect for me to walk into. However, two individuals that want to be together will both make any changes needed to make that happen. Having been let down by Peter during our marriage made me feel he at least owed me honesty now and lying to me made me feel he was still unsafe to be with.

What hurt the most was being told I had cancer, and that is obviously enough in itself. I just felt Peter was thinking about himself again. I was so angry. I didn't have much contact with him after that, until later that year.

David continued to take me to my hospital appointments and we fell into being together again. I think, over the weeks of various appointments and the diagnosis of cancer, I didn't want to go through it alone. I knew I would need support and as David had been the closest person to me, I wanted him to be the one to help.

Anyway, the MRI scan showed a large lump in my left breast. My own consultant was away, so it was another doctor who gave me this news. I was also told that because of the size of the lump, I would need a mastectomy. This is something I didn't want and my consultant had told me previously, that because I have large breasts, she could do a lumpectomy. I relayed this to the other doctor and she asked me what cup size I was. I told her I was a double-F, and she then confirmed that I would indeed be able to have a lumpectomy. I had to have another biopsy and the lumpectomy confirmed at my next appointment.

That second biopsy was so painful. What hurt the most is that they pushed down really hard after doing it and it caused a lot of bruising. At this appointment, the nurse mentioned about routine mammograms. I'd just received a letter for my first one whilst going through the ordeal of being diagnosed. I'd rung the breast screening unit to cancel the appointment and told them why. The nurse, at this appointment, told me how lucky it was I had found the lump due to the fact that the routine mammogram would not have picked it up because apparently, I have dense breast tissue.

It was just a matter of weeks between me finding the lump and the appointment for the mammogram. It's scary to think such a large lump would have been missed. My cancer was just about to spread, too. Being aware of our own body is so important; if it wasn't, I may not be here now writing this to you.

After the MRI and second biopsy, it was confirmed I had breast cancer and needed an operation. After receiving that news, David took me out for the afternoon, to a place called Oulton Board. We had a walk around and went into some of the lovely little shops there and he bought me a heart shaped pebble with the words, *'You're Amazing'* written on it. I put it in my coat pocket. It was weird walking around back then, looking normal but knowing I had cancer.

Soon after, I was invited to go to a Ballet performance with two of my lovely clients. I can remember sitting in the audience, looking around, thinking and wondering, *"How many other people are sitting in here with cancer?"*

It was now early April 2016 and my operation for the lumpectomy was booked for the beginning of May. I could have had it slightly earlier, but I owned a Healing Centre and I needed to make some changes to get ready for this cancer journey.

Dear Lisa

I decided to close the Centre because I didn't know how long the treatment would take. I had to clear it all out before my operation, but my clients were lovely and very supportive and were impressed with how positive I was being.

Each step of the way I didn't worry, but instead responded to news as I was given it. Don't get me wrong, I was naturally upset and became more so each time I went to the hospital after receiving more bad news. However, I needed to sort out the practicalities of my life and work and I didn't have long to do that. David was very supportive and helped me clear out the Centre and prepare for the operation.

I never thought I was going to die, even though my mum had died and I'd been diagnosed with breast cancer at the same age as she had. Actually, my cancer developed when I was forty seven, which is the age my mum died. What I did find difficult were the effects that this process and treatment had on my body.

I had my lumpectomy on May 9th, 2016. David took me to the hospital for my appointment which was in the morning. I was given a heart shaped cushion, from the hospital to use after the procedure, which was to protect my breast afterwards, by placing it under my arm. I was a bit nervous about it, not so much the operation itself, but that weird feeling of being put to sleep and then waking up again with something having been done to you.

I remember, as I started to wake up, I could hear David talking to me. "I'm here, Yummy One," he was saying. He calls me various different names, but most involve being yummy. My favourite is 'Yummy

Breast Cancer

Scrumpets'. I call him my 'Yummy Man'. Hearing his voice then was so lovely.

I've had a general anaesthetic only once before and I cried as I woke up, so it was comforting knowing David was there after this one. For all the upset in everyday life that I've had with David, there are times when he really is supportive.

My sister lives near the hospital and she came to see me. It was so lovely seeing her, always so supportive and there for me, that it meant so much. I feel incredibly blessed to have her in my life. We've always got on but this experience brought us even closer.

I went home after the operation, on the same day. David was amazing, helping me wash and getting me anything I needed. But now the sad part comes...

All the same issues of not feeling important, not being put first, not having enough time for me and being left alone, all returned. A day or two after the operation, David spent the whole day polishing his van. Tom came to see me, though, and he looked after me and cooked dinner.

By the end of the day, I felt upset because I was feeling neglected by David. I wanted him to be with me and the longer the day went on, the worse I felt. As the weeks passed, he obviously had to work, but he would return back to me so late in the day. I did have friends and family that came to see me, but as always, I needed more of David. I just never seemed to have enough of him and that feeling has never gone away.

Before my operation, we talked about getting engaged and we even ordered a ring that he told me was ready to collect afterwards. Now, I'd just had a lumpectomy and was awaiting the results to determine what further treatment I would need and I wanted David to make my world brighter, to bring me joy. But he didn't do it. He didn't go to get the ring. He didn't arrange anything to brighten this time for me, instead leaving me just waiting for him to be there.

I arranged a weekend away for us, but unfortunately, it didn't go too well. The Sunday before we were due to go away, we went to a nearby country hall for lunch. A tree house sat amongst its beautiful, manicured gardens, and it would have been the perfect setting for him to have presented me with the ring. The subject came up and David said to me, "I haven't picked it up yet." I got upset and we argued. "I don't want the ring now or you either," I told him.

You would think, knowing we were going away the following weekend, that he would have made the effort to get the ring and make that weekend amazing. After all, it had been his excuse for not having it yet. He thought he would be giving it to me on the weekend away. So, that weekend, we arrived at our hotel and soon after he told me, "I still haven't picked up the ring." I'm sure you can imagine how I felt. I was so upset and angry, that I made him go to pick it up the next day, of which I spent walking along the beach until he arrived back.

All the time I've known David, I have been upset by feeling that he puts me last, thinking he always has too much else going on in his life. He *is* under pressure and so much gets in the way of him focusing on me, especially when I really need him. Actually, the most hurtful thing is that when I really needed him to focus on me, he didn't. I always felt, and still do, that his order of priority is his car and van, his life, his children and then me.

Anyway, after the weekend away the stress between us continued, so I rang the well-being service. We both attended a weekly group-talk about stress. It didn't help *us*, but it did show me that my stress was being caused by something *in* my life, showing aspects of my relationship were making me feel unhappy. At the beginning of July, I felt so unhappy and stressed that I told David to go.

I was half-way through cancer treatment at this time and had been told the cancer was just about to spread because I had a tiny part of it in the first lymph node. This put me border-line for needing chemotherapy. It really upset me because I didn't want to have chemotherapy, unless I really needed to.

My tumour was sent to America to be tested to see how border-line I was, whether high or low. The result wasn't either, but was somewhere in the middle, and so my consultant agreed I didn't need to have the chemo.

My cancer was oestrogen positive, so I was given the drug Tamoxifen, to block the oestrogen and prevent a reoccurrence. I also had to have four weeks of radiotherapy which started in the September.

The stress and upset I experienced when being with David, was worse than if I'd been on my own and continued the cancer treatment without him. I wasn't alone because I had friends and family to help me, many of whom offered to take me to my radiotherapy appointments. This made me feel very supported and more relaxed.

Dear Lisa

On Sunday 24th July 2016 I went to an afternoon tea dance and met a man there called Joe, who actually lived quite near me. On 18th August 2016, nearly a month after meeting this man, I wrote this in my journal:

"At the dance on 24th July I met the most amazing man. He is like an angel who has been sent to rebalance all the hurt and mistreatment I've been through."

I have also written a list of the things he rebalanced and this is the list:

He put a picture on his phone of us and then of me.

He takes pictures of me when we are out.

He changed his plans for going away, because he wants to spend time with me.

He drops everything to be with me, if I need him or I'm upset.

He constantly thinks and acts to make our time together special.

He cooks for me.

He makes me tea.

He buys me flowers and my favourite chocolate.

He does everything he can so I am happy.

He opens the car door.

He holds me.

He makes our time together so meaningful, seeing all the opportunities to make our experiences magical.

He expresses his love to me.

Breast Cancer

He looks at me deeply.

He is always one step ahead of me. He never leaves me waiting or wondering if he is going to give to me. He is always thinking of me and putting those thoughts into action.

I also wrote that he is my moment in time, somewhere in time, journeying together with the most beautiful experiences. I felt so loved and looked after.

The reason I called him my moment in time, is because he is just over twenty years older than me. I know many people have big age gaps in relationships, but I want to grow old with someone. I don't want to increase the chances of being left alone. I felt he entered into my life at this time, and for a period of time only. I did tell him, "This will not have longevity." Unfortunately, he wanted to be everything to me, but he knew he couldn't. He couldn't change his age and therefore, *couldn't* be everything to me. Sadly, this then caused a lot of problems. He would try to make me feel insecure, so I'd end up needing him more. Insecurities in him surfaced and if I ever talked about my past and what happened to me, he couldn't bear the thought of me being with someone else.

One night, after he'd been drinking, he became quite abusive. I was so scared that I locked myself in his bathroom with my phone, and texted *"HELP"* to Peter. I only texted that one word because I had little signal and didn't have my glasses, so couldn't see clearly to write. Thankfully, Peter came to get me and took me home. There were quite a few times before that incident which also felt very uneasy.

On another occasion, when on a day out, I'd been feeling unsettled by how things were between us. I told him I would rather just be friends, but it didn't go down too well and he started being verbally abusive again. It was horrible.

As we were walking back to the car park, I put my hand in my pocket and felt the heart pebble that David had given me. I'd forgotten it was there but feeling it in my pocket made me reconnect to all my positive qualities. I thought of the words inscribed on it: *'You're Amazing'*, and it was as if that little pebble, right then, repelled all the negative horrible things that were being said to me.

I didn't want to go home in the car with Joe and I didn't have Peter or David's number anymore, because he'd convinced me I shouldn't keep them. So, I rang my son instead and told him I needed picking up. This calmed the situation and I agreed to let him drive me home, which was okay.

I got Peter and David's number from Tom later that day. I was glad to be home again, but it felt such a shame that what had been a lovely relationship became abusive. I know I've had a lot of upset with David, with the lack of focus and feeling unimportant, but he's never been horrible to me. He always tells me I'm so precious and lovely.

So, while I was going through four weeks of radiotherapy, I was also, once again, in an unsettled relationship. The radiotherapy ended on 19th September 2016 and the relationship ended at the end of December 2016. Again, going through cancer treatment is definitely enough to deal with. Radiotherapy is really harsh and by the end of the four weeks I was

Breast Cancer

very burnt and sore. It was immensely draining and I felt so tired.

I was quite upset, before I started the radiotherapy. I'd a client, who'd also been through it and she told me that I would have tattoo dots on my chest. This allows the radiation to be given in the correct place. One of her dots was right in the middle of her cleavage. Instantly I thought, *"I don't want a dot there, to be seen whenever I wear a low-cut top."* I already felt mutilated after the surgery, all bruised and swollen, with a massive scar. It was obviously healing, but I didn't want to be left with 'dot-to-dot' boobs.

I rang the hospital and told them I didn't want the dots and they put me at ease, explaining that I would have three dots, one in the middle and one each side of my body. All would be low down and would be covered by the band of my bra. I felt much happier about that and now I hardly even notice they are there.

When I started the radiotherapy, my dad and step-mum took me. I was very fortunate because there is a centre at the hospital which gives support to cancer patients called the 'Big C Centre'. I went there before my treatment. It's a lovely calming space where you can relax and have a cup of tea. It was strange going in there for the first time with my parents, though. Looking at my dad and step-mum, we were asked, "Who is the patient?" It was a weird feeling that I was the one having cancer treatment, yet I was the youngest.

After the radiotherapy was over, I attended a six week course, run by Macmillan. It was called the 'Hope Course' and was design to help with life after cancer treatment. It was very valuable and was lovely to be with other ladies who had just been through a similar experience.

One of the things that was covered on this course was that once cancer treatment is over, everyone else thinks that's the end of the cancer journey. However, the effects of cancer carry on for much longer, for years or even life. I can understand this as it took over three years for my breast to stop being really painful. It's only in this last year that it feels more comfortable and doesn't get as swollen.

Two years after I finished the radiotherapy, I regularly attended training days and have now become an Emmett Practitioner. One of the things I learnt and received was a lymphatic treatment, which made a huge difference to the swelling and pain in my breast. However, it *is* still tender if too much pressure is applied but the scar is much less visible now.

Some other horrible effects I had were as a result of taking the Tamoxifen. What an awful drug that is. I didn't ever want to take it because I hate taking tablets and I would have preferred to treat myself as naturally as possible. When I took the first tablet, I sat on the bed and cried. The side effects were awful and my body couldn't cope with having radiotherapy and Tamoxifen at the same time. I'm surprised it's not advised to wait before taking it, once the radiotherapy has finished.

I had to stop taking the Tamoxifen for a couple of months to allow my body to recover and after a few months, the side effects became less. However, I did completely stop taking it in November 2019 because I could feel it was causing me problems. The drug basically put me in a fake menopause where my periods stopped and sex was becoming very uncomfortable.

I took Tamoxifen for three and a half years and it took a whole year for things to start feeling more normal again. I was advised to take it for ten years but I dread to think what state I'd be in if I took it for that long. I feel so much better mentally and physically for not taking it anymore.

I am helping myself though. Now, I only eat organic meat and dairy, as mass produced meat has hormones in it. In January 2019, I started doing the Keto diet. I've eaten a low carbohydrate diet for a long time, but I was struggling to keep my weight stable due to being on the Tamoxifen. I found the Keto diet excellent. It's basically a very low carbohydrate and high fat intake and I lost about six pounds very easily and found I could keep my weight stable, too.

The other significant thing by eating this way, was the effect it had on my temperature control. I would become very hot because of the Tamoxifen. It wasn't hot flushes, just a high body temperature, and soon went back to normal. I also found the "foggy brain" went away, too, which is another symptom of menopause.

When I stopped taking the Tamoxifen, I went to the doctor to have the over-fifties well-being check. I'd never had my cholesterol checked before, or my blood sugar levels and after eating a high fat diet for nearly a year, I was interested to see what level my cholesterol was. It turned out that it was very low, in a good way. My sugar levels were okay, but on

Dear Lisa

the higher end of okay, which slightly surprised me. However, my nan and mum both had diabetes.

I still eat a very low carbohydrate diet with a good level of fat. I'm sure the years of eating low fat weren't good for me. It is funny that the recommended diet to help prevent breast cancer, is how I *used* to eat. I think, although I was always thin, that my body probably had higher sugar levels and lacked the essential nutrients I needed from fat. I also think that eating a low carbohydrate and higher fat diet works well for me.

I don't worry about getting cancer again. I obviously don't *want* to get it again, but neither do I want any illness. I don't worry about dying, because I know I will die one day. I'm more interested in quality of life and not longevity.

So, Lisa, 2016 was quite an eventful year. I started 2017 with David back in my life, after five months of no contact. I contacted him shortly after ending the relationship with Joe.

Enough Time

19th June 2020

It has been nearly two weeks since writing. On Wednesday 3rd June I went back home for four days. I wanted to give my house a thorough clean, to get it ready for when I started working again in July. I also went home to have some "me time".

David's birthday was on Saturday 30th May. Unfortunately, the weekend of his birthday wasn't stress free and I was upset because we didn't have much fun time together. This was because he spent time messaging people about buying his old van. In the end he didn't sell it but traded it in when he bought his new van.

Each day that weekend, we only spent two hours where we went out for a walk in the forest. I was upset because this amount of time is not enough for me.

Dear Lisa

We only get every other weekend to go out and do things; that's just four days a month we get to spend together, though we do go for walks in the evenings.

I don't think he considers that I spend many hours amusing myself because I'm on my own and don't even have my work at the moment. I *am* okay amusing myself, but I want to make the most of the time we get together. Even when we see each other at weekends there are still chores that need doing, which is okay, but there needs to be enough time for fun together, too.

After being upset and the stress causing my tummy to be bloated and uncomfortable, we both agreed I needed to go home to focus on myself. Those four days at home were really good. I went home on the Wednesday morning and by the Friday morning I had lost five pounds. My tummy was feeling so much better, too. Obviously, it's not possible to lose that amount of weight in such a short time which is why I think the stress must cause fluid retention that affects my abdomen.

I spent the four days cleaning and sorting. I felt so much better physically and so much happier, with no stressful thoughts. I spoke to David every day which was good and made me feel happy. I drove back to his house on the Sunday, arriving just before he had to take the children home, so I got to see them for a short while. I stayed there while he took them back, so I could unpack my things.

On that following Monday morning, I weighed myself to see if my bathroom scales were the same as David's, relieved to find I was still nine-stone. Two days later, with my tummy feeling uncomfortable again, I weighed myself and I was nine-stone, five.

Enough Time

Over the last two weeks my tummy has continued to feel really uncomfortable, but things *have* been stressful again.

The stress has been over not having enough time, *again*. I become very upset with the things David says to me when we're trying to discuss what is wrong and how to make it better. He's happy with how things are in his life, busy with his time full of things to do, but it's not the same for me. He has so many more commitments than I do, which take up a lot of his time. I have always wanted him to reduce his commitments, so we can have more time for us, but it never seems to happen.

Obviously, the children will take up regular time for about seven years yet. I *am* ok with that, if I get enough quality time, too. I've lived my life for the last thirty years, by having a good work-life balance. I believe life is for living and enjoying, which is probably why I'm feeling so unhappy. I feel I'm not enjoying or living my life as I want to, yet I have always done that before.

I spoke to a lady from the well-being service today, which was very helpful. The outcome of that being that relationship counselling may benefit us, either with David or just by myself. I also talked to her about complex PTSD and having a treatment called Eye Movement Desensitisation and Reprocessing (EMDR). This was mentioned to me after I had cancer.

Unfortunately, the NHS don't offer EMDR for childhood trauma, because it requires more sessions to be beneficial. They only help adults who have just experienced a one-off traumatic event. It's ridiculous really, that I can be helped physically but I can't get help mentally or emotionally. Help *is* available for a one-off experience, but no help is available for going through years of abuse. That actually, in itself, causes issues because being abused is a very lonely place of self-survival. It's a place where help is desperately needed. Eventually, when you *are* able to ask for help, none or little is available. That just adds to the feeling of not being worthy, of just being left to suffer.

The people who only need a few sessions don't have to pay. It would cost them so much less than someone like me, who needs many more sessions, but has to pay. They pay nothing and I'd have to pay over a thousand pounds. How is that balanced or even fair?

Things that are obvious just seem to go unnoticed, like actually treating the cause of something rather than the symptoms. Why, in this day and age, are we still treated as individual parts with the physical, mental and emotional areas not all being linked together? Yes, this is known, but still not properly acted on to enable treating a person as a whole. I know mental health is progressing, but there's a long way to go and lack of funding for it. The focus always seems to be on the physical and keeping the body functioning to keep someone alive, but people die because of mental issues and feeling unable to cope, hence suicide. Surely, what's important is that being alive means *feeling* alive, with the desire to wake up every day to live.

I would like health care for every area of my health. I would like this care to support me being healthy and not to just fix what is broken in some way. I would like health care to support every aspect of me.

Enough Time

Basically, I would just like to receive the support I need to help my physical, mental and emotional health. I don't mind paying towards it and I do pay towards my care where complementary treatments are concerned. People have been paying me for over thirty years to support their well-being. I would just like to see more of a balance, so that more people get the support they need.

It was suggested that I ask the Sue Lambert Trust if they have contacts for EMDR, but I think first the relationship counselling is more needed. It was reassuring, talking to the lady from the Wellbeing service. She made me see the things that affect me due to my past, are different from what I am feeling in my relationship. She confirmed that being in the wrong environment will cause stress and I'm trying to be okay with things that just aren't right for me.

I told her, "I understand how to live a balanced life and for me, much of that is obvious." I do understand it isn't like that for everyone and some people need more guidance than others and I don't expect my partner to know what to do or to be perfect. But I do want us to be able to listen, understand and work together in a constructive way.

Maybe I *am* with someone who is happy with everything in his life. Let's face it, he gets a lot of me and he *is* doing what he wants, with me supporting him in those things. I think he's content with me just being there and fitting in to the structure of his life. My own life is different where I spend much of my time waiting for him, for his attention to be more focused on "us". With him, I feel like my life is very chore-based. I still have work-life balance, but with him the chore-fun balance is out of sync.

Dear Lisa

I often say, "A sorted life still takes quite a lot of time to maintain that life." There is work, of course, and even without work there's cleaning the house, cooking, tidying, washing cars, gardening, maintenance, decorating, food shopping, all the things that need doing just to exist. The more we add to this, the less time we have to relax, have fun, enjoy ourselves and be able to have experiences and adventures.

It's so important to me to make time for each other, to have that quality time enjoying each other's company. If I don't have that in my relationship, I feel disconnected to my partner. It feels very empty. It feels like we're just existing instead of living life to the full together.

Counselling

22nd June 2020

I'm sitting in the garden. It's a lovely warm day. I rang Relate this morning, but all they did was give me the number of a local counsellor. I can see all the local counsellors on the Relate website so I've decided that when David gets home, we will choose one together. My reservation about having counselling is the more self-development I do, the further away it seems to put me from having similar values and beliefs from someone. I do, however, think there must be other people out there who *do* have similar values to me. Maybe my problem is that I continue to accept what isn't right for me.

I always see the good in people, that everyone has potential and the power to make a good life. I think I end up trying too hard to get the balance, knowing I can only do my part, with the other person needing to do their part also. There must be a reason why I keep returning to what I don't like in the belief it will be different, but it never is.

Dear Lisa

I feel there's an element of safety being with David and perhaps I'm afraid that if I meet someone new, they will let me down, too. I think I need some "me time" because, at the moment, I do not have the strength to deal with filtering through men and encountering more who are only focused on what *they* want. This keeps happening, and each time I go back to David.

I'm hoping that having some counselling will help to either make the changes needed to be with David, or for me to be able to choose what is right for **me**. I want to be able to stay strong and focused and not be wobbled if I meet the wrong people. Instead, I want to be able to calmly see what's not right for me and just say, "No".

Home with ABANDONED

14th July 2020

I've not written anything for about three weeks. It's been a very interesting three weeks however, with many changes, and I've discovered a lot.

Two days after I last wrote, I came home and decided to stay here permanently. Once again, I was feeling upset. After asking David to make enough time on our next weekend together, he didn't, and that's the reason I came home.

I've decided against having relationship counselling, but what has helped me is listening to speakers online via a trauma conference. This is useful in my work but has helped me personally, too. The part I connected to the most was the talks on empaths. I already knew I was an empath but hearing how they are in regard to relationships, has given me a vital

Dear Lisa

piece of information, which is that empaths always see the good in people.

I've said, so many times, "I do not see the negative in people." Although I do see where their lives are at in the present moment, I don't focus on that. Instead, I see that everyone is amazing, capable and powerful. I see they can create something extraordinary, turning anything around to make things better. I don't see what needs correcting, but I *do* see what can be achieved.

You may think that's a good thing, but it's actually not been good for me. *I* have seen what can be done to make improvements, but *they* needed to be willing to put effort into making the changes. So, I ended up being life coach in my relationships, with my partner fighting me all of the way most of the time. In the end it has never been okay, because it hasn't come from inside of them. They were still disconnected to their power and magnificence.

What I *have* realised is that I have to stop entering into relationships with people like that. I have to stop being their coach. I need to allow myself to be with someone who is self-aware and recognises their own strengths and weaknesses. They need to be able to look after themselves in every area of their life. If we can't look after ourselves properly, how are we able to look after each other?

I will always see people as amazing and capable, but from now on I will also see how they function in their life at the present time. If we are miss-matched, it is our individual responsibility to handle our own lives and make any changes needed.

This reminds me of a programme I saw on the television, where a man wanted to marry a lady. He

Home with ABANDONED

knew he needed to make changes to be good enough for her. After about a year of doing what he needed to do, he felt he could now offer her something that she deserved and he proposed to her. That story has remained with me simply because I think it's wonderful that he recognised what he needed to do and even more importantly, he went and did those things.

Like mistakes, it doesn't matter where you *are* in life, but instead, what you do about it. It's in the actions that make life as it is. Think it, see it, acknowledge it and do something about it. It's when people don't feel powerful that they fail to do something about it, but everyone is powerful and capable.

It's been great for me to see what I've been doing at the very start of a relationship; actually, even before it becomes a relationship. I see the signs; my heart and gut instinct tell me the things that aren't okay very quickly. Instead of saying, "No, this isn't right for me," I stay and try to work with the person to make it right. But not anymore. I have written on a piece of paper, which I've put on the fridge so I see it daily: *"Follow your heart and be led by what feels good."*

Being home on my own has helped me see things clearer. I'm happy here. I don't stress myself out and I meet my own needs. I love my life now. I've looked at how successful the rest of my life is, to see what I've done right, to create such balance, so I can do the same in having a successful relationship. What I've discovered is what I've just told you.

When my life just involves me or things about me, like work or things I want to do, I have always followed my heart and gut feelings. I've been led by

Dear Lisa

what feels good. I've walked away from things that haven't felt right. I've created a good, self-sufficient life where I am very good at looking after myself. This has worked in all the areas of my life, so now I'm going to do that to find a life partner.

I suppose the relationship side has been more complicated because it involves another person. I try so hard to work with them, but whether it involves another person or not, the principle is still the same: follow what feels good and walk away from what doesn't. I wonder: how many other people are ignoring these valuable signals and messages that are given to steer us along in life? I think many of us hear them but choose to ignore them.

I have doubted that I'm correct in what I am thinking. My fear has told me information to keep me in the situation, which is actually not what I wanted to hear. Fear makes me scared to be alone, thinking I won't be okay. It keeps me disconnected from my power and greatness. Then, I think it's better to stay with what I have. By doing that, I completely ignore all the positive messages, ones that are actually going to guide me and enable me to make my life what I want it to be.

Fear is in my mind and in my thinking and I can think all sorts of silly things which aren't real at all. What *is* real, however, is the instant gut feeling I have.

Now, what I'm doing, is staying with what feels okay and comfortable and walking away from what feels *un*comfortable and not right for me. It really is that simple. It only gets complicated when my over thinking gets involved and starts analysing everything, which just ends up leaving me confused. It's

Home with ABANDONED

no wonder I feel this as many people have said my heart is saying one thing and my head another. The way is to listen to the heart and give this information to the head. My mind then tells me what I need to do in order to achieve what I want. That's how the head and heart work together. The heart is about what I want and the head is about how I achieve it.

This probably sounds easy and actually it is, as long as I *see* my fears but don't let them control me. I therefore decided to take some time to think about my fears in regard to my relationship with David.

I asked myself, "What is holding me back; what is stopping me from leaving and staying away from the relationship with David; why am I constantly leaving and returning, and then, in the process, preventing myself from being with someone where I'm happy?"

I wrote as many fears down as I could think of, then, I wrote the opposite of each one. I've put them on the fridge to remind myself and I read them every day so I can strengthen them in my mind. The fears I wrote are:

Nobody will look after me

I will be alone

Nobody will truly love me and value me

Nobody has the same values and I'll be alone, again

Having written I'll be alone *twice*, clearly shows that that's my biggest fear. It's interesting because something happened recently which connected me to my inner child, **ABANDONED**.

After writing my fears, I wrote these positive affirmations:

I will be looked after

I will be loved and valued

There are other people who do have the same values

I will have my companion

I know that with affirmations they need to be written as if they already exist so I have written:

I am worthy

I am truly loved

I am looked after

I am valued

I am respected

I have a loving and supportive husband

I am happy

I am living my life fully

I have a secure place

I have a balanced, equal adult relationship

I trust the universe and everything is okay

When I read them, I feel strong and confident that I will not accept anything less.

I am focused now on following my heart. I'm acknowledging my fears but *realise* they're fears and they help me to be there for myself. It's like I said before about my inner children: I am getting to know them. I am listening to them, which allows me to see the value they hold and what I need to do to be there for those parts of myself.

I discovered **ABANDONED** when Peter came to see me last week. He told me he's seeing someone.

Home with ABANDONED

We talked lots, and we cried. He said that he would always be there to support me and that he would always love me, which made him cry even more.

There have been a lot of thoughts that I've kept to myself and not told Peter about, but I did tell him what I felt. "You need to think about what you actually want and what your heart really desires," I said, and added, "If you want something then you have to actively go and get it." Out of fear, he hasn't done that. Instead, he needed me to create a safe environment where he felt wanted by me. I knew he needed me to stop seeing David.

I reminded him of the card I'd written for him years ago, which he presented to me earlier this year. It basically said how I loved him, only wanted *him* and was completely committed and dedicated to him, which I totally was. Before he presented the card, he asked me, "Do you mean what you say?" "I always say what I mean," I replied. He then gave me the card to read, but I don't think he was expecting the response he received from me. I looked at what I had written, probably about six years previously, and I thought, *"Yes, that is exactly what he had from me, but the problem was, I didn't get that from him."* That is what I told him.

What I wished he'd done was shown me the card and told me how lucky he was to have had that and to say sorry that he hadn't given that to me. Instead, he questioned me to see if I'd meant it. He only had to look at my past actions to see that not only did I mean it, but I always behaved in a loving, committed and dedicated way. Peter's fear of not being wanted meant he couldn't see how much I wanted him. That led to him giving me away and causing me a lot of damage and pain in the process, something a husband should never do.

I told him why I could never go back to him and that it was because *he* needed to make me feel wanted, not the other way around. I could never go back to him until he stood in front of me, offering himself with love, protection and dedication. He needed to come to me as a partner. Instead, he is only ever there as a friend who constantly doubts that I want him. If he presents himself as a friend and keeps telling me he doubts we could ever repair what happened, then of course, we can't. I don't need him being there for me if he's still afraid that I don't really want him. I can't go back to that. It was that belief that told him he wasn't good enough for me and that I didn't really want him, and so that led to him giving me away.

I told him, "It's not my job to come to get you because I'd just be going back to the same problem." He needed to *prove* he would be there for me. He needed to show me he wasn't afraid anymore, but he never has. He's looked at *my* actions rather than his own. All he could see was that I kept choosing David and going back to him. Therefore, in his mind, I wanted David and not him. I also told him, "The reason I go back to David is because he turns up wanting to be my partner." This makes me feel wanted and safe with David because I know he would never share me.

Peter assumed my actions meant I didn't want him, but in our marriage, it was *his* actions that didn't want *me*. So, however difficult it was for him, it was *his* job to make things right and finally present himself with all the qualities he actually received from me. Only then would I have felt safe to return

Home with ABANDONED

to him. I cannot return to a scared man. I will only be with a man who shows up in strength, knowing what he wants and is not afraid to come and get it. That type of man will offer himself and his life, which I can then choose to enter into, if it is what I want, too.

I think many people are afraid of rejection, but we all have a choice and we have to allow people to be free. After I had expressed my feelings, I said to him, "There's nothing I'm asking you to do other than take some time to really feel and think about what you really want, and when you do, you can take action to get it."

I don't know if he truly does love and wants me or if he wants someone else. I allow him the freedom to do what is right for *him*. If I try to control or manipulate someone to be with me because that's what *I* want, it will never really be harmonious. It's a wonderful feeling knowing that someone is freely choosing to be with me. Rejection doesn't feel nice, but it's not a bad thing. It's actually kind, because then I'm free to be with someone who actually *wants* to be with me.

REJECTION is just another inner child which I need to be there for. I can tell that part of me, "You don't want to be with someone who doesn't really want you. It's okay not to be wanted, because there are and will be plenty of people who *do* want you." Being truly wanted feels lovely. It's never going to feel good being around people who don't really want me, and I don't actually want those people in my life anyway. I can tell **REJECTION,** "It's okay, I'll make sure your life is filled with people who want you. I want you. You are always welcome here to receive the love and reassurance you need."

Dear Lisa

The next few days, after I saw Peter, I had a horrible feeling. It felt like grief, but somewhat different. I sat with the feeling for a while and realised that feeling was abandonment. I knew Peter hadn't abandoned me and I know he will also be there if I need him now. I did tell him he needed to focus on his new relationship because that's where his focus *should* be.

As I recognised **ABANDONED,** I welcomed her and started to listen. She showed me all the times in my life that I'd been abandoned, which was emotional abandonment. My mum left me when she left my dad to be with my uncle. She didn't take her children. She may have wanted us, but my dad wanted to keep us which I'm so pleased about, because my abuse would have been so much more.

I was only five years old when my mum left. When I went to visit her, I wasn't allowed to call her Mum outside so that people didn't know her business. I wasn't even allowed to call her Mum at home, either. I believe my step-mum found it difficult that my dad had an ex-wife.

As my parents had other children, I have never truly felt a part of the family and I still find this difficult at times. They had their own proper family units and I didn't fully belong to either of them. Just writing this upsets me.

I have felt alone for so long: alone for years surviving abuse, alone by not really fitting in with my family, alone by not being included, and alone in not receiving the emotional support I needed. I received the physical care where I was clothed, fed and nurtured, but I've been so alone emotionally as I grew up, and even as an adult.

Home with ABANDONED

When I had cancer four years ago, I saw how much my dad loved me. He and my step-mum really supported me then; they were there for me. My relationship with them has been better ever since. I know they are there if I need them, but they still aren't there regularly. My dad never contacts me to see if I'm okay, even though I know he's always happy to have contact with me.

Tom and I don't have lots of contact with each other, but I feel it's my job as the parent to make sure I contact him if we've not spoken for a while. I'm happier knowing my dad is there for me if I need him, but I suppose I still feel forgotten about sometimes.

As I listened to **ABANDONED,** I realised the way things are with David are a reflection of how I grew up. David is there for all the practical help I need. However, in everyday life I feel abandoned because even when he *is* there with me, he isn't actually giving me his full attention. That's why I feel like I'm the maid, living a life of chores with little intimate attention until he wants something from me. So, a lot of the time I feel on my own.

As I saw all the times that I'd been abandoned in my life, I asked, "How do I abandon myself; how am I not meeting my emotional needs?" The answer was that I didn't remove myself from people who didn't meet my emotional needs. I had learnt to protect and respect myself, but I hadn't seen that I was abandoning myself as well. All of this is about me standing up and saying no to what is not right and then walking away. I told **ABANDONED,** "I will now be there for you. You're not alone. I'm here and always will be. I won't let you be in a place where you're not being emotionally looked after."

Dear Lisa

I've done so well protecting myself from physical harm. I don't give myself away, in that way anymore. Now, I can see that I also needed to protect myself from being emotionally harmed.

The feeling of abandonment I have had before is a feeling much worse than grieving. In grieving there is a release with crying, but tears didn't come to help **ABANDONED**. In the past I've made the uncomfortable feeling of abandonment go away by going back to my relationship with David or trying to find someone else. I never listened to **ABANDONED;** I just pushed her away by feeding her some comfort food, which was unhealthy. This time, with listening, understanding and knowing how to be there for myself in that way, it instantly made the horrible feeling go away and stopped me feeling abandoned.

A week ago, I told David I only want to be friends. I'm actually on my own more at home now, but I am happy and don't feel alone. I can have people in my life in a way that works for me. I still talk and see David, which actually works better as a friendship. I don't need the same things from my friends as I do a partner. I've been enjoying going out walking with my other friends and I feel happy and free.

After seeing Peter, I did a 'letting go' ritual. I wrote on separate pieces of paper that I let both Peter and David go. Then, I burnt them on the fire. I know letting go means allowing things to be free, to be there or not to be there. Letting go of something at the right time, creates and allows these areas of my life to flow better. We have to let things go occasionally so they can return again at a better time that's right for us.

Perception

24th July 2020

I've had a busy ten days since I last wrote. I finally went to the hospital for a CT scan and thankfully I have no tumours in my abdomen or pelvis, so there is nothing seriously wrong. I think the upset I was experiencing was causing the problem. I *am* still having symptoms, but I hope they will settle soon. I am trying to relax now I'm back at home. I think it will take some time, though, especially as there is still some upset.

David and I are trying to be friends, but he finds it difficult when I go out for walks with a male friend. I've told him he needs to choose either to be friends or have nothing. Unfortunately, both of those choices are difficult for him. It didn't help that after he was stressing at me over a walk I had with a friend, I joined a dating site. This has upset him even more, but I've tried to explain that I want a life with someone and as much as I care for him, life for us just

Dear Lisa

doesn't work. Neither of us has another partner, so we can still enjoy a friendship.

The problem David has is he doesn't stay focused in the present moment but worries about me finding someone else. I've explained to him that there is no one else right now, so only worry about it if it happens. Being realistic, both of our lives will move on at some point. It doesn't help that he has a very negative mindset and believes he doesn't have any opportunities to meet someone. He can't see he has just as many opportunities as I do. I trust and believe that person is out there and it can be scary not knowing when and how I am going to meet them. But I do have faith and believe it will happen. In the meantime, I focus on life in the present moment. I make any changes, if needed, and enjoy where I am at now.

I had another conversation with Peter earlier today. He mentioned again how I didn't want him, but instead always wanted David. After all I told him a few weeks ago, he just can't see what I'm saying. This time, in very simple terms, I said to him, "I always wanted you. I thought I'd spend the rest of my life with you." And then I reminded him, "It was *you* who didn't want *me*." "I did want you," he replied. But it was him who gave me away. I told him to go and write down somewhere, "Anji has always wanted me."

The perception Peter held was created by his beliefs and that's why he could never see I wanted him. Whatever I did would never make a difference because he needed to recognise how he perceived things. I know my perception, at times, has caused

Perception

me emotional upset. It took me some time to recognise I could seek another way to view a situation.

I had a client this week who was upset over a family member. Their behaviour has caused a separation between other members of the family. As I listened, I could understand how this person was hurting. The trauma experienced in childhood was causing them feelings of being unloved. I know how experiences can create a void and a sense of something lacking. The feelings I had created a perception that there is not enough love, and at times, it was very painful to see others receive attention. This perception made it difficult to see the love that *is* there.

Some people behave in a way to alienate others. My behaviour was either being upset or to distance myself. It's so sad really, because my pain actually wants to be loved and included. My perception of my family situation often caused me to be separated from them. I've always felt alone with my pain, scared to tell my family how I feel. I always felt that nobody would actually be there for me. I knew I couldn't stand up for myself as a child, and I felt nobody would stand up for me either. So, I kept quiet about being abused which made me feel alone and abandoned.

I'm learning more and more to listen to those hurting, unloved parts of myself and hearing what they need from me. I've realised there's a very big difference between being emotionally triggered when everyone around me is actually meeting my needs, to being triggered in an environment which is *not* meeting my needs. Both things need changing and both need inner child recognition.

Dear Lisa

When I *am* emotionally triggered, even though my needs are being met, this indicates that I am holding beliefs that will cause me to never see what is actually there. As an adult I can sit with myself and see that my needs are actually being met and then ask the question, "Why do I feel this way?" Using Peter as an example, the answer to that question would be, because I believe I'm not wanted. He can then look back in his life to the times when he felt that way. He can reassure himself now that he *is* wanted, by seeing who is actually there, wanting him.

In contrary to this, when I'm emotionally triggered and my needs are *not* being met, the process is the same but more action is required. This is what I am doing by learning to keep myself safe, both physically and emotionally. As an adult, I am now capable of removing myself from situations that are not meeting my needs, thereby only allowing myself to be in healthy environments. I do still need to listen to my inner children and beliefs, however, to give me the knowledge of how to do that.

The interesting thing I learnt from listening to my client was how it was affecting her. She's a very balanced, together lady and was obviously hurting from what was happening to her. This showed me that you don't have to have experienced major trauma in your life to feel the same pain as someone who has, and that's because we all have each inner child, albeit with different amounts of how happy and content they are. So, when a situation arises, it's natural for some inner children to surface because they are not feeling okay. Inner children come for loving attention. They need the parent part to look after them and make them feel okay again.

Perception

I have said at times, "Because of the things I've been through, I especially need to be treated with love and respect." I now realise whether I have suffered or not, that I should be treated with love, respect *and* kindness and I should not allow anything less for myself.

When I think about meeting someone new and telling them about my past, I do have to remind myself that my past doesn't matter. I stand here as a beautiful, loving, caring lady who should be treated well. Clearly, I still believed I didn't deserve to be treated with love and respect and I needed them to understand what happened in my life as a reason for them to give me that. I will tell someone about my past, but only when they begin to love and respect me for the person that I am and for no other reason.

When I am there for myself with love, respect and protection, my inner and outer worlds will feel balanced. All my inner children will live in harmony, all content, and knowing they are all equally loved and valued.

Dear Lisa

Alone

27th August 2020

It's been about a month since I've written, and in that time, I've had a few ups and downs.

I've just had a phone call from David which has resulted in us completely going our separate ways. It's really hard to let him go completely and not have him there as a friend, but it's still upsetting when he's here. With him going I feel so alone, like I have nobody there for me. I know I *do* have people there, but they have their own lives. Tom, my son, is there for me, but he's very busy. However, he is always there if I need him.

I'm finding it difficult with David gone because I need to go to the hospital. I had a colonoscopy last Sunday. He took me to the hospital and looked after me so well, but now, I don't know who to ask to help me. I need to go back because they couldn't see everything clearly, and I'm seeing the consultant next week to discuss it further.

Alone

David helped me with so many practical things too, which of course he can do quickly, if anything needs doing. I will just have to get used to having someone else do the things I can't do for myself. I know it's going to be hard without him, but in time it will be easier and I don't have to be upset by the things I don't like anymore.

I've had over eight years of emotional turmoil. I've never been happy being with him, but he saved me from what was happening with Peter. Seven years after Peter brought David into our lives, they are both now gone. They have been there for me all this time in some way, yet somewhere inside me, I felt they *shouldn't* be there. I think I just couldn't bear to be without someone loving me. It still really upsets me being alone. It helps by reading the positive affirmations I've put on the fridge, especially the ones that read: "I trust in the universe", "I am present in this moment" and "I am looked after and everything is okay."

If I stay present in this moment, just with this day, then I see I am okay. I am resourceful. I do have my son and I do have friends and family that care about me. I believe I will receive the support I need, as and when I need it. I am feeling quite calm with a sense of positivity that I will be alright. I'm sure I will be upset at times, after all, that's only natural.

Dear Lisa

I am enough

23rd September 2020

It's been an eventful three weeks since I last wrote. I suppose to sum up what's been happening, I have had some lovely days out with good company. Also, I've been focusing on how people fit into my life and the level I have with them. When I say 'them', I mean men.

The last time I wrote to you, I said David had gone, and Peter, too. Things were upsetting me. Now, both Peter and David are back in my life. I *am* having less contact with Peter, however, and that's made me feel better. I allow him to be there, on the periphery, as a support for each other if needed.

I am enough

David and I obviously care about each other. He struggles taking the relationship hat off and putting a friend's hat on and finds it difficult to let me get on with my life. This means he stresses and tries to interfere with the things I'm doing. It's a real shame because he then stops himself having an enjoyable friendship. I know it's not easy adjusting and I find things difficult at times, but at this present time we can still be there as friends. So, I've had lots of conversations with him and most importantly, I've stayed strong and firm in what is right for *me*.

Last weekend, David helped me decorate my bathroom. We had a really lovely time and it felt so nice to be at ease together. I did, however, feel a bit unsettled on Monday and spent some time reflecting on why. I realised that although I get on with the men in my life, not one of them feels right to be with. There is always something good with each person. However, like with David, there is nobody in my life right now where my gut feeling tells me it feels good in a relationship kind of way.

Peter rang me on Monday and I told him, "I am not feeling okay." He tried to point out all the fun times I've been having lately, basically trying to help me see the positive things in my life.

This is the mistake and misguided advice that is often given. It's why, at times, mindfulness practices do not work. You may have heard about being grateful for the things in your life? This is called the Law of Gratitude. It can be a very useful practise to help see all the good things and creates a much more positive frame of mind. However, all the mindfulness and positive focus tools can become a distraction

Dear Lisa

from actually accepting what is present. Actually, I did this unintentionally on Monday with myself.

When I woke up on Monday, I was feeling unsettled and quite emotional. I got myself up, showered and ready for my day. My plan was to paint the bathroom after David had done all the preparation over the weekend. Doing the first coat actually made me feel better because I was focusing on the painting. When I'd finished, I had to wait for the paint to dry before I could do the second coat. This was when I started to feel unsettled again.

I made myself a cup of tea and sat in the garden and whilst there, I took the time to listen to how I was feeling. I couldn't actually pinpoint what it was, but I knew it was about things not feeling okay. Then I reminded myself about some of the things that haven't been okay in my life, especially when I was a child. Basically, I took the time to acknowledge those parts of myself. Then I realised the feeling I was having now was because things didn't feel right like I said earlier, with the men in my life.

None of this made me feel worse, though, and actually made me feel much better because I'd listened to myself and seen clearly what wasn't okay. I then felt strong and connected to what *is* okay for me and what I want, and, most importantly, staying steadfast in that. It means having a few conversations with these men to make myself clear, which will allow them to make a choice whether they want to accept the friendship knowing it will not be anymore. I'm actually looking forward to the day when my gut feeling and my heart feel excited about someone in a relationship way again.

I am enough

If I'd sat in the garden thinking about all the good things in my life and not listening to my inner-self, all I would have done is shut the door on what needed to be listened to. I often write about bringing light to the darkness and this is what I mean. These parts of me feel dark because they are shut away and ignored. This in itself can cause depression, because I have literally depressed my feelings.

I explained this to Peter and he did understand. I also said, "Just because I'm upset or not feeling okay in some way, it doesn't mean I'm still not connected to all the good things in my life. I am still very grateful for all I have. I still acknowledge all of those things, but I acknowledge *everything* that is present." How many times have we all heard about acceptance? Does anyone really understand what that means? Well, to me, this is acceptance, the acknowledgement of what is present and allowing it to be there.

I will only feel balanced and settled when I see the bigger picture. I can't just focus on one aspect, but I have to acknowledge *every* aspect, and I'm doing that, not just with my feelings but with every aspect of my life. Then, each part of my life will receive the level of attention it needs in order to be balanced.

So, focusing on being happy again as quickly as possible, doesn't actually *make* me happy because I achieve happiness by loving *all* the aspects of myself. As each part appears, I allow them to be there. I listen, understand and take action if need be.

Sometimes, no action is required and this happened the other day. I wasn't feeling too good and it seemed like my inner children were running around trying to think of who could make me feel better.

I realised I was looking outside of myself thinking, *"Where can I get fed from so I can feel better again? I am not enough."* I wasn't there for my inner children or myself, because I didn't believe I was enough. What a great realisation that turned out to be. Instantly, I told myself, "I *am* enough." My inner children then stopped searching for the one to make me feel better, and I felt like I was holding them, as I was being there for myself.

I have heard, so many times, about being and feeling whole. Well, I finally felt what that was. I felt whole and complete because I realised that I *am* enough, being truly there for me, able to love myself. So, on Monday when I was feeling unsettled, I didn't once look outside of my own being. I knew I was enough. All I needed to do was give myself some time, draw the uncomfortable feeling closer to me, so I could truly be there. Then, I understood why I didn't feel okay.

I know it can be scary because these feelings do feel uncomfortable, but that is normal and natural. Most importantly, I've learnt that it feels better to welcome these uncomfortable emotions. Feeling my pain won't kill me. If I allow it to be present, that part will show me the answer to what I need and let me restore the balance again. These feelings would only kill me if my deepest, most hidden pain is not seen or not brought into the light and does not receive the love it so desperately wants.

Love will transform everything. More and more I'm learning not to withhold that from myself. I know that the times I have felt suicidal is because of the lack of love my pain feels, whether that's from myself or from another. The pain that's unbearable

I am enough

is not actually the pain itself, but the hurt of not receiving love. It feels better when I draw this pain closer, because love makes everything feel better.

So, you can see, I have discovered quite a lot over the last few weeks. I believe life is a journey of discovering and understanding who I am. I can do this a lot easier if I realise that I will still be okay by accepting the pleasure *and* the pain that surfaces in my life. One of the spiritual laws is called the Law of Flow. This is a great law because it shows me that things are always flowing. Basically, nothing stays the same. I am in a constant flow, so I may feel unhappy today, but on top of the world tomorrow. It only becomes a problem if I fight what's there and push against it.

I'm going to finish for today and will write again soon. I just want to say again that realising I am enough has made a huge difference to how I feel and allowed me to be there, for myself, even more.

Dear Lisa

Inner Strength

6th October 2020

The last two weeks have gone really quickly. I've felt quite low over the last week, but I've not been out much and I'm missing my nature walks. It's been very windy and raining a lot, and I'm hoping the weather will be brighter soon when I can go out with my camera and take some photographs of all the autumn colours.

I've been back to the doctor again and will be having another blood test. The low mood I'm having may be because of my hormones and being in the menopause. I won't be able to have any treatment because of having had breast cancer, but I have enough skills to be able to help myself naturally. I eat a healthy balanced diet and I know many different mindfulness techniques, my favourite being dance and walk-

Inner Strength

ing in nature. Now I also know how to be there for myself. I can accept I'll have down days and I'll give myself what I need, even if that means spending the day just watching the television.

I felt quite emotional at the beginning of last week because I had a client who had to cancel due to feeling unwell. I felt very unsettled, which resulted in a really bad sleep that night. The next morning, I still felt emotional, so I knew I needed to stop and take a moment to listen to what was going on.

A few inner children surfaced, one being **SELF-RELIANT** and the other, **ALONE**. They told me that if I can't be self-reliant, I will have nobody to look after me. Being this way is a good thing, but I created my **SELF-RELIANT** child because I believed nobody *would* look after me or be there for me. I reminded my inner children, "You do have people that love you and who would support you if you ever needed them too." Then I said, "I will seek the support needed so that your needs are met." I also reminded myself that I do actually have enough. I'm earning enough and everything is actually okay. Once I had given this attention to myself, my mood lifted and my inner child, **HAPPY** was able to surface. I had a very good day after that, feeling content and balanced again.

I was also particularly emotional at the end of last week, too. I didn't feel okay for three days, with Saturday being a very low day. I realised I was feeling trapped in an unhealthy situation with David and that for the last three months, I'd been trying to help him see that he has a choice of whether he stays and has a friendship with me or doesn't. If he wants a friendship, then I ask that he focuses on the time he

Dear Lisa

has with me, rather than worrying about what I'm doing with the rest of *my* time.

Unfortunately, he continues to stress and be controlling, which keeps unsettling me. One minute I think we're having a nice friendship and the next he's stressing and being opinionated about what else I'm doing.

On the Sunday just gone, he started questioning who I may be seeing this week, with suggestions of different male friends. He knows I spend a lot of time on my own and he wasn't at all concerned that I had a nice week planned. Instead, he just worried about any threats which may happen and therefore take me away from him. What he doesn't realise is I've gone from having a relationship with him and now I am his friend.

I've gone back to what doesn't work for me over and over again, but this time I'm not going to. If he wants to make changes, he could get some guidance, but I don't think he wants to do that because that takes effort.

Anyway, after feeling very uncomfortable about him questioning me and after he'd gone home, I suggested we have no contact for a couple of weeks. He wasn't happy as I knew he wouldn't be because it will be really scary for him not knowing what I'm doing every day. I'm hoping this time it will break the need for him to know what I'm doing all the time. Maybe then he can relax and enjoy a place in my life. I've had some texts from him, saying *"Things aren't okay and it's all shit."*

I've personally felt so much better. I feel free and most importantly, whether I feel happy or not, I will look after myself. I think because I'm there for my

Inner Strength

inner children like I never have been before that I'm actually feeling very balanced and strong. I suppose building a relationship with my inner children, understanding and meeting their needs, is creating inner strength. I feel I have so much more inner strength now than I ever had before.

It's incredible how powerful it is just taking some time to listen to my inner children, to understand and then be able to give the reassurance needed. I hear many times that we need to let go of these so-called negative feelings, to focus on being positive, and I know that these feelings, in turn, will lead me to the positive. They will never go away because they are an extremely valuable part of me. These are the parts that know what I need. They hold great wisdom. When I listen, I can then be there for myself and meet those needs, and the more I do that, the stronger I become.

When I was looking through my journals in preparation to tell you about the last seven years with David, it was fascinating reading them. I've written them over the last eight years. Reading the same things repeatedly through the years has made me see how my journey has been. Now I can look after myself in a much clearer, healthier way. Reading them enables me to see my confusion and I can now see how I wasn't being there for myself. I was looking for something outside of me, to help me and make everything feel okay. But it's helped me to see and learn that *I* am the person I need to be there for me to meet all my internal needs.

Dear Lisa

Letter about David

10th October 2020

It'll be a week tomorrow since I suggested to David that we have no contact for a while. He's actually messaged me every day and we've spoken at the end of most of them. However, the normal routine of when we used to message has changed. I've felt so much better because I have felt free to get on with my life. I do care about him and would have liked him to be there as a friend, but this last week has shown me how his behaviour and the things he says creates disharmony and a stressful environment.

Letter about David

I found this letter in one of my journals which I had written to myself in July 2016:

"Dear Anji

I'm writing this letter to remind you of how you are feeling right now and how you've felt over the last few weeks.

You've tried to have a relationship with David many times now and each time you end up feeling unhappy, worthless, and not good enough.

Yes, you love him, but being in a relationship with him just doesn't work. There is so much attention and effort at the start which soon diminishes to a level you are unhappy with.

What you want is someone who is more proactive in your time together, who loves to touch you, cuddle you and just be natural. Someone who can prioritise what they need to do knowing what attention is needed for you.

David is a good man, but his way of being doesn't suit you.

You always feel you are waiting around for him.

The car obsession will always drive you mad.

The fact that he struggles to get up and go out in the morning and then has less time in the evening, his lack of time management, will also drive you mad.

Remember the level of closeness, hand holding, head stroking and being held will always reduce to a level which will make you feel unhappy.

You have to tell him to do everything, like he can't think for himself, although he can do that when you are not together or when he's trying to get you back.

Dear Lisa

You have to stop this cycle because you've done it too many times.

You have to be brave and let the things or people go that drag you down.

Of course, you will need to adjust, but you will be okay and you will stand up in this universe and say, 'I am worthy.'

Worthy of great things, of a true love, commitment and dedication, of a relationship you know is possible to have.

Stand up and say, "No more will I allow others to treat me in this way." Follow your heart and do what feels good. If you had a job you didn't like, you would change it.

Spend a long time with someone first to see if being with them is a happy experience before embarking on a relationship with them. People soon show their true colours.

So, give yourself time x"

It's four years since I wrote that letter and it reflects on everything I am saying now. Back then, I was clearly missing something to stop me repeating the same pattern for another four years. This letter and my journals show that I knew what wasn't okay and clearly, I wasn't able to carry out what I needed to do.

It's taken me the last four years and especially the last two of those years, to get to this point of seeing things clearly and being able to be there for myself in a way like I've never been able to do before.

The missing part was that I hadn't acknowledged my inner children. I've been building a relationship

Letter about David

with all these different aspects of myself over those last two years, listening to them and learning how to meet their needs and give them healthy attention which creates balance, inner strength and peace. I know I am enough and I *am* all I need, which has enabled me to say no to what is not right for me.

I met David in 2013 and wrote that letter three years later and have continued to write them for another four years. I tried to escape this cycle so many times that I've lost count. The last seven years probably only continued for so long because I kept leaving the relationship and giving myself a break from the upset. David would be there giving me attention, and after a few months I'd go back to him. Then, a few months later, I would be unhappy again.

I spent time with other men in the hope of finding someone new and for so long I just needed and wanted someone to rescue me from this repeated cycle. Deep down, I knew it was *me* that needed to be the rescuer. But I wasn't capable and didn't rescue myself from the situation with Peter. David did that, so I didn't learn how to rescue myself from him, either. Without developing those skills, I just remained vulnerable and easy to manipulate. Now that I *have* learnt to be there for myself, I have now saved myself from this unhealthy cycle and can be prevented from entering into something else that is emotionally unhealthy for me.

Dear Lisa

Progress

24th October 2020

Last night and today, I saw how different I am now. Since I came home in June, I've been trying to maintain a friendship with David. It's been a real struggle and very stressful because he's still trying the same old things, so I go back to him. I allowed him to come to see me yesterday evening and we agreed to go for a walk on Sunday. But on the condition that if he can't just focus and enjoy the time with me, then I will not see him again and there will be no friendship to be had.

I think he realised that I'm not going back to him. Not long after he left, he sent me a text saying, *"I am not going home because I can't face spending the weekend alone."* Years ago, he sent a similar text, and back then it really unsettled me. This time, however, I *knew* he was trying to unsettle me, perhaps hoping I would wonder where he was going instead. But I didn't feel upset this time, although I didn't like it. Instantly, I felt myself become strong;

I was there for myself, for the part that didn't like it. I emotionally felt self-protected and safe, knowing I don't need something outside of me to make me feel better, and especially not from someone who is trying to unsettle me. I didn't reply to his text and soon after he rang, several times, but I didn't answer his calls either. He continued texting but I just ignored them.

I've been in this cycle for too many years. I've been honest and clear and offered a friendship, but that hasn't been working either. It's scary letting things go that are not good, things that will leave me feeling alone. I realise now, that stripping these things out allows **ALONE** to surface, so I can seek to bring in the new and healthy. Now I know I am never alone because I am always here and in turn, I can make all my inner children feel supported.

Other people can also make my inner children feel supported, happy and safe. However, they can also make them feel *un*supported, unhappy and unsafe. I will not do that to myself. If other people try to do that to me, I will not allow them to.

I felt a bit emotional this morning but was taken out for a lovely lunch where I laughed a lot and now, this afternoon, I'm feeling bright and energised again. I've organised a walk with a friend tomorrow which I'm looking forward to, and I'll be taking the camera to capture more of the beautiful autumn colours. It's a lovely feeling knowing I have friends that genuinely care about me. It's also a comforting feeling knowing I can keep myself safe with anyone who *doesn't* genuinely care about me.

Dear Lisa

Back at David's House

16th November 2020

I am actually writing this from David's house. The Monday evening, after I last wrote, David turned up at my door. He announced he wanted to get some help, to work on the things that need changing because he loves me and wants to be with me.

I don't know if we can be happy enough together but I do feel, with counselling, we will find out for sure. If we can't be together, I think it will help us

Back at David's House

both to accept that and move on. I try to move on, but David never goes away. I'm going to see what progress is made over these winter months, and as we're both single, we've joined a bubble for this current lockdown. I'm only spending the week at David's and I felt that being here would allow me to focus on writing to you.

Whatever I go through, I never lose my drive and I'm always proactive. I'm like this because I know it's up to me to make things happen. I'm in control and know I can do it. I have a lot of energy and am prepared to put the effort in if I need to. One of the frustrations I have with David is how he doesn't get on with things unless it involves something to do with a car.

I was thinking earlier today about how he came to see me to tell me about him getting some help in order to try and make things better between us. In my proactive way, I have been the one to suggest people for him to ring. He has seen someone once, but it was somebody I know and we feel it's best he sees someone else in case we need to go together. I've emailed him a list of counsellors to ring and so far, he hasn't arranged to see anyone. I've decided he needs to be the one to sort this out. And this is where I feel bottom of the list. He's busy with work but I also know if he needed to ring about something car related, he would've done that by now. So, I'm going to leave it with him. If he wants to be with me, he will sort it out.

Dear Lisa

Self-Care

19th November 2020

Since 2017, when David came back into my life, I have been continuing to focus on looking after myself. I've tried many times to have a life with him, but now I realise it is never going to work while there are too many things that need addressing. David is a good person but he lacks responsibility, and therefore his priorities are not in order. I have tried to help but I realise now, unless he wants to make it different, things will not change.

This isn't just about how David is in the relationship, but also how he is in himself whether I'm here or not. I've always asked him to sort out his finances. Unfortunately, he will prioritise what he wants to do over what he *needs* to do, and I simply will not get into debt to have what I want. But he will. If I had debts, I would manage and clear them first before buying the things that I wanted. I would buy what I needed, but I wouldn't spend thousands of pounds on a new car if I couldn't really afford to.

He doesn't seem to realise that the interest he pays means he's paying so much more. If he cleared the debt, he'd soon save to have what he wanted or at least be able to borrow sensibly. I discovered today the full extent of what he will do to get what he wants, something that's caused him to waste an extortionate amount.

He's also lied to me and bent the truth. For years, he's basically prioritised the need and want for his perfect car. As a result of this, his finances have suffered, time with me has suffered, as has his role of being a responsible parent. He couldn't see that if he'd focused on sorting all his debt out six years ago and spent a few years clearing it, he would have paid so much less in interest and would probably own his car outright, too.

Knowing he will even put what he wants above his children, has clearly made me see why I struggled for so long to be happy with him. It didn't matter how much he loved me; he always put himself first, above everything. For me, this is never going to feel comfortable to be around.

I'm not upset by what I now know, but I am shocked. I also felt connected to my inner child, **STRENGTH**. Now, I clearly see this is all about him. It hasn't impacted on me, and my inner children feel just fine, and that's because of the inner child work I have been doing with myself.

I've just decided to make a cup of tea. I'm feeling very thoughtful right now, because of what I've been telling you. Before I split up with David in June, one of the things I asked for was a water filter. His kettle gets a lot of lime-scale which ends up in the tea. He didn't want to get one however, saying it was a waste of money, and that at some point he wants to install a water filter. This upset me because the jug water filters are so cheap. It made me feel worthless at the time.

Anyway, being back here again and seeing the collection of new shoes and several smart speakers he's bought himself just shows me how he thinks about himself and gets what *he* wants. Oh, did I mention the new car he bought, too?

He did, however, de-scale the kettle because I was coming to stay. So, as I was just making the cup of tea, I couldn't help but feel a bit upset as I thought to myself, *"What am I doing here?"*

I'm here because he said he will get some help. I will monitor what is acceptable for me every step of the way. I'm still living my life *my* way, and I'm happy with that. That, in particular, is my focus. There's a lot that needs to be different if we're to have a relationship again. I don't know if those things will change, but we *can* be a support to each other, and in the meantime, I'll continue to care for myself and make the choices that feel right for me.

Over the last three years, I have focused more on caring for myself. I've slowly been allowing the parts of myself to come out from a dark hidden place and into the light. I've listened to these parts intensely and it's still an ongoing process, but now I know how to look after *me* and bring loving attention to myself. I now have a much wiser inner parent.

A really big shift happened with me in February 2019 and this is what I wrote in my journal on 23rd February that year.

"Return to me.

Twenty years ago, I didn't listen to my gut intuition.

Twenty years later, now I am listening.

I feel like I have been lost for twenty years and now I've found myself again.

So, what have I been doing? I was not listening to my gut.

My intuition, my knowing is felt in my tummy area.

The Vagus nerve is said to be like a second brain. It feeds information, reacting and feeling, knowing what is and what isn't okay.

Unfortunately, all too often, the mind kicks in and spends time analysing the information that the Vagus nerve provides. Fear kicks in, then conflict and confusion are felt. At this point, fear wins the day and I do not act on my gut reaction or intuition.

My mind tells me a story from all of my insecurities that hold me back to the place in which I am: my comfort zone, even if it's not really okay for me. The intuition, gut feeling, my seat of knowing, is always correct. It is the one reliable source.

It's simple to be me. It's simple to walk the journey of life if I listen. The knowledge in my head is there to use, to carry out the actions when I have the knowing from my gut feeling. So, what does this feel like? It is the first words I internally say about something. So many times, I hear this internal voice, but all too often, I ignore it. Ignoring it leads me into situations that just don't work for me.

Dear Lisa

I find myself by making choices from my gut feeling. It's a very powerful place to be, a place where I will only accept what is right and okay for me, and I will not accept anything less.

The body connection is so important. It experiences everything, guiding me constantly. But I just don't work with it very well at times because I don't listen enough.

The way to live in balance is to be connected to my body, because the body has the answers. It tells me what is and what is not okay for me. It also tells me when to rest, if I'm eating the right foods, about my exercise habits, or lack of them and what I need to change.

Now I am listening to my gut feelings, I feel free and I feel like myself. I'm excited that my life is full of good things and that more good things will keep coming. It will be all good things because I will not allow what I don't like or don't want.

I am in charge. I am in complete control of my life.

But if I listen to my mind, I will so often not be ok."

I wrote this when I wasn't in the relationship with David, once again trying really hard to move on from him. We didn't have much contact but occasionally we spoke or had an odd text. He started seeing someone who he actually didn't want a relationship with, but he then seemed to disappear. My inner child, **NEGLECTED**, found this very difficult and left me feeling emotional and unsettled. If I texted him, he wouldn't reply until later the next day, something he'd never done before.

Self-Care

I wanted him to come and see me because I felt seeing him would make me feel better. At this time, I hadn't discovered **NEGLECTED**, so I wasn't able to feed myself and give myself what I needed to feel better. I was looking outside of myself and I thought David was the food I needed. But he refused to come and see me, which just upset me more. I asked my friends for support, which helped. However, it didn't make me feel better because *I* needed to make it better for myself. This happened just before going away on a three day walking trip with Peter.

So many times, when not with David, Peter and I often had a trip away. We still got on well and enjoyed holiday times together as friends, and always had a good time.

I told David I was going away with Peter. While I was away, he sent me a text: *"You are so precious to me. I am worrying you will be intimate."* I ignored it. It made me so angry with him because he didn't seem to care when I needed *him*.

I was in contact with a couple of friends whom I'd asked to help me stay focused. I was feeling really unhappy, experiencing an empty, neglected feeling, and it felt so painful. I just didn't know at the time, how to help myself. I obviously wanted the pain to subside; I needed attention and I was getting it from Peter. I felt safe with him and being intimate with him, after all that time, was actually okay. The problem was it only helped a little bit, just enough for me to be able to carry on and live through the neglect.

I'd left a pair of shoes at David's house which I needed back at some point. In the April of that same year, a few weeks after being away with Peter, I was exhibiting my work at a healing fair in Norwich. On the second day, David turned up with my shoes. As he approached me, he burst out crying and I took him to one side so we could talk. He told me he missed me and loved me, and in response I said, "I'll contact you later because I need to get back to my stand."

It was after this point that I tried, really hard, not to run away when things were difficult between us. I was hoping this would give us the opportunity to talk about what wasn't working and to make things better together.

This brings me back to near the beginning of this letter, when I started to tell you about my inner children. Staying in the relationship longer allowed them to surface. At this time, I started letting them be there, realising I needed to listen to them, as all the previous journaling had given me a way to express what was inside of me. It took time to understand it all, but it did lead me to eventually see what was needed.

Lisa, I'm so glad I've written all these things down. I can see my journey of discovery and see that I was still missing a vital part, which actually allowed me to finally be there for myself. The connection to the gut feeling was so valuable and although I wrote that just over eighteen months ago, having the focus of doing what felt right for me enabled me to listen to my inner children; my fears.

The final missing part was *working* with my inner children. I needed to understand how to be there for the fear in my mind. I needed to understand that fear, the value and wisdom that it holds. It's not a dark part of me but a part that was *in* the dark. It was rejected and hidden away, desperate to be seen,

Self-Care

heard, held and loved. Once I started drawing the fear closer to me and listening to what it was saying, I then knew what I needed to do.

We are told to love ourselves, to relax, be positive and do mindfulness activities, but we never seem to be taught how to love ourselves. In my opinion, fear has been misunderstood and been pushed away in the rush for happiness. Fear just needed to be embraced, to realise it isn't scary at all, but instead, is what leads us to happiness. This is what I have discovered.

So, I have been actively listening to my gut feeling and my fears, which I see as my inner children. By listening, I've built an inner strength and I now have a valuable tool to keep myself safe. This will guide me along the journey of my life with whatever that brings. There will be ups and downs of course, because that's life. There will also be days I may feel down and just want to stay in and watch films most of the day. But there will be more days, many more, where I will feel bright and active. All of those days are fine, because on each one, I will be listening and will give myself the care I need. Even when I'm having a bad day, I will feel good, because I know I will be looking after myself.

There is one more inner child I want to mention again. I told you before that I had felt suicidal many times. My inner child, **SUICIDAL**, has not been present for quite some time now. I realised this the other day and it shows me the inner changes that have occurred. I also know, if she does surface, I am able to comfort her. What has been present, so much more, is **HAPPINESS** and **EXCITEMENT**.

Dear Lisa

This letter doesn't have a happy ending, but it doesn't have a sad one either. The end does not come until the day I die. Now is the present moment of my life, a life that unfolds each day at a time. I will journey the rest of my life listening, knowing that the answers I need to help myself, are within me. I know an outside fix will not save me or rescue me, because that could lead me to make an unhealthy choice. With my inner strength and wise inner parent, I can, and will, feed myself with all the good, healthy, wholesome stuff.

I've told you about my personal journey, which has been helped because of my professional journey. Both my personal and professional lives have taught me so much and I have trained in many more therapies since we last had contact.

My Career

20th November 2020

Lisa, you know that from the age of thirteen when we were at school together, I decided then what I wanted to do for a living. I remember thinking about it because of having to choose what subjects to study at school. I knew then that work would be a big part of my life. So, I told myself, "You need to pick something that you will enjoy doing every day." And from there, I decided I wanted to work with people, helping them feel good about themselves.

Once I left school in 1984, I studied massage and beauty therapy for three years at the West Suffolk College, and when I qualified, I moved to London to live with Mark. Being in London enabled me to work with some experienced therapists, and this taught me many more skills. My interest was always doing the treatments that helped people with their specific problems.

Dear Lisa

When I returned back to Suffolk nine years later, I started working for myself. I was twenty-eight years old then. I attended more holistic courses which included reflexology, reiki and kinesiology. The kinesiology was to help with emotions and spiritual guidance and I started to run self-development workshops. I was doing all this whilst being in contact with you. Since not seeing you, my training has continued and now I have many tools to help many more people.

I love the way my career has evolved and the different teachings I've been drawn to. About seventeen years ago, I went to a mind, body and spirit fair near Cambridge, and whilst I was there, I saw a man demonstrating the way he massaged. It wasn't really a demonstration, but a treatment like I'd never seen before. I was mesmerised. It was the most loving thing I'd ever seen. The treatment was a NO HANDS® Massage and it was being carried out by the founder, Gerry Pyves.

I simply had to learn how to do this, so I signed up and spent the following year doing all the relevant courses of Foundation, Practitioner and Advanced Practitioner. I then spent the next four years attending the Mastery Programme, which took place four times each year. I took my Mastery exam after these four years, and to my delight I passed! That was twelve years ago now and I'm still the only Master in this region, which is a bit annoying because I'd love to be massaged more often myself by a Master.

The reason why I dedicated so much time and money to become a Master was because I wanted my clients to receive a masterful touch. It truly is one of the best things I have ever learnt and is the basis of

My Career

all the treatments I do. It's quite hard to explain it but because I use my arms, rather than my hands, the touch feels more encompassing. Touch is very powerful and this training taught me to deliver it in many different ways to achieve the clients' outcome. The only way to really understand NO HANDS® Massage is to feel it because there really is nothing else quite like it.

After I'd mastered my touch, I wanted to further my training around the spiritual laws and self-development. I trained for a couple of years with the Diana Cooper School and became a 'Transform Your Life' therapist and teacher. I worked with this for a number of years, running workshops and one-to-one sessions.

After I had cancer, I discovered the Emmett Technique. I attended a one day course which is designed for everyone to learn how to release muscle tension. It came at the perfect time, as I'd just finished my radiotherapy and still had a restriction when I lifted my arm, due to the surgery. After this one day of learning eleven moves, I was hooked and spent the next year learning and attending the practitioner course.

I love the Emmett Technique because I can use so many of the moves on myself. Adding it to my treatments is also amazing. The technique is light, so pleasant to receive and easy for the practitioner to do also and fits well with all the other therapies I do.

I use the Transform Your Life and the Inner Child work with people to help them mentally and emotionally, whilst working with my massage treatments, too. For ten years, I hadn't had much involvement with the NO HANDS® Company. However, last year, Gerry ran a Trauma Discharge Therapy training course, and what was so interesting about this was that my work had already evolved in that way. What has made a big difference to the way we massage is the neuroscientists have now proven and discovered what our touch is doing to the body and to the nervous system.

We aren't working any differently and we know the effects our clients have, but now we know why. It's nice to know what's happening and to have that scientific evidence. To be honest, though, all I care about is how my client feels at the end of their treatment. Their reaction is evidence enough for me, and them, too. All people want is to feel different and much of feeling different is the support and care they are receiving.

So, my work and treatments have evolved into helping people with any type of pain, whether that be physical, mental or emotional. I understand so much more about trauma, both from traumatic experiences and the trauma created by everyday life, from the things we see around us or in news reports. I also understand more about fear, emotional pain and the inner children. Most physical pain is caused through mental or emotional pain, and I now understand that inflicting pain on to a client would actually increase their trauma levels. That's why I love the Trauma Discharge Therapy and The Emmett Technique so much. Both are highly effective and feel comfortable to receive.

I have actually been hurt before when receiving a massage treatment. The outcome from that massage was tears, and I thought to myself, *"I have suffered enough pain and I don't want to suffer anymore."* A

My Career

massage treatment should be a pleasure, not a torture. It is so important that each client is always in their comfort zone. I also use the touch to help the inner children with a 'Mindfulness Inner Child Massage'. This is about bringing loving attention to any inner children that surface. I also show my clients how to do this.

I forgot to tell you that I also did a Forest Bathing Course which is about being mindful in nature. I love nature so much, Lisa. I help people to engage with it, using their five senses to be fully present in the moment. I walk often and take my camera with me to take mindfulness pictures. Nature is such a gift, and wonderful for helping trauma, because being in nature means slowing down, therefore calming to the nervous system. It is definitely essential for my well-being. A walk in nature is very different to a *mindfulness* walk in nature. A mindfulness walk is much slower and I can easily spend two hours not walking very far because I'm spending time being fully aware of what is around me.

My other passion is dancing. I created 'Transformational Dance' about ten years ago. It's based around the elements of Earth, Water, Fire and Air, and allows for self-expression, freedom and movement to create a greater connection to the self. Whenever I dance, my mind stops thinking. My body takes over to move and create the dance, perfect for the moment. It's incredible when you *feel* a dance, rather than think it. The dance that is created is amazing, totally unique and wonderful.

I love my work and I always remember a very lovely lady once saying to me, "You don't just do your work but you live your work." I feel that too, and

Dear Lisa

it's always been important to me to practice what I preach.

Bye for Now

21ˢᵗ November 2020

Well Lisa, I think I've told you most of what my life has been like since we last saw each other. I'm sure there are many more stories to tell, but what I wanted to share with you are the things I've been through and all the personal growth I have had. Writing this letter to you has been the icing on the cake. It has given me a platform to express and finally bring the clarity that I needed.

It's been wonderful writing to you since May, just over six months now. It's funny, because I started writing to you during the first lockdown whilst staying at David's house and now, I'm finishing it in the

Dear Lisa

second lockdown, again, at David's house. As you read it, I'm sure you can see my confusion at the start and my clarity at the end.

I wrote the letter to help myself and it's been a journey of discovery, of what feels like the last piece of the jigsaw. Now I know how to love myself and be there for me, to keep myself safe, both physically and emotionally.

Throughout this whole letter, I have imagined you reading it and visualised us meeting again. I see us having the biggest hug ever. I know that would be so emotional, but in a good way, and just thinking about it is bringing tears to my eyes. I really hope that is the outcome of this letter and I really hope you forgive me for not looking after you and our friendship.

The other outcome, I hope, is that many people will now understand how to love and be there for themselves. I hope people see that it doesn't matter what life has been before, but what matters is where they are now. The past experiences can empower and give strength to make now and the future better. I hope people realise, life is a journey, day by day, which can incorporate all sorts of things. I hope they see that *they* are in control and have the strength and self-care to make every day be okay, even when it doesn't feel okay.

Thank you, Lisa, for the friendship we had and even though you don't know it, for being there over the last six months.

It's time to say good-bye, but I hope by saying this, I may get to say hello again one day.

Bye for Now

Take good care.

I love you my dear friend.

Forever in my thoughts,

Anji xx

p.s. It's Thursday 10th December 2020. I just needed to tell you one more thing. Last night I had my inner child, **LOST,** surface. She is present because David is unable to stay in my life. I made it clear to him that I just want to be friends and I don't want to be with someone who is immature and puts his desires before his responsibilities. He will only be my friend, however, if I don't see anyone else. But I am. It's sad we can't be friends and that we have to lose everything, and this is why **LOST** appeared.

I had quite an emotional day yesterday. Last night I took some time to connect to the pain I was feeling. It's pain and upset that I've had before, and it led me back to David. But this time I knew the pain needed me, and soon I saw **LOST**.

LOST is wandering around a big forest and looks so alone. I welcomed her into my arms and told her that I'm here. She told me about all the things she had lost: her mother, her place, her innocence, self-respect and self-worth, and even some friends. I told her, "You are not lost anymore. I have found you and you have found me."

I see all the things she had lost and I said, "I understand how painful it has all been." I know she loves the forest and she loves getting lost there. She feels at ease in the forest because I'm always there with her, keeping her safe. Whenever I go to there, I wander around to explore and never worry about being lost.

Dear Lisa

I realised, when I'm there, that I connect to **LOST** and together we feel so happy, safe and loved. Now that I have consciously connected with **LOST**, she feels closer to me and today I am less emotional. In fact, I'm actually feeling settled and balanced again as the day goes on.

It's incredible how listening to myself and meeting my own needs has on feeling okay and being able to cope. It is actually healing and each time I do that I become stronger. The more I listen to myself, the more I discover about myself.

Connecting to **LOST** means she's not alone and lost anymore. She's now in the light, receiving the loving attention that she needs. This makes her feel content and valued. Before, she never felt that way because I kept feeding her with something which I thought I needed from someone else. Of course, someone else *can* give to me, but they can also take away. I will always give her what she needs. I will give all my inner children what they need.

I do, however, feel that my journey with David is still not over. I also feel I still have much to discover about myself. My eyes are opening, and the more they do, the more I will understand my own self, my reactions and my fears. All that I see will give me the ability to love myself more.

I will write again to share with you all I discover.

SELF-HELP GUIDE

Dear Lisa

Introduction

Once you have read my letter to Lisa, you can refer to this self-help section for a reminder of the things you can do to help yourself.

You may want to re-read the letter occasionally to remind yourself how to communicate with your inner children and how to be there for yourself.

The aim of this book is to help you build a relationship with all parts of yourself. The change you will make is reconnecting to all of you. When you are disconnected you will feel unbalanced and that unbalance won't necessarily be in your *whole* life, but with *parts* of your life and how you feel. You may find there is a dysfunctional area or an aspect of your life that doesn't feel harmonious in some way.

You reconnect with yourself by building a relationship with your inner children, listening, understanding and acting. You will see the value of all parts of yourself and you will learn how to work with each part to enhance your life, meet your needs and be able to cope in any situation.

You don't have to let go of anything and actually, that is scientifically impossible anyway. But what *is* possible is to change the form. You are transforming how you feel by building a relationship with all of

Introduction

yourself and by understanding all the parts *of* yourself. This, in turn, enables you to love and be there for yourself.

There are so many dysfunctional relationships that exist, and that's not surprising when we are not building healthy relationships with ourselves.

You are capable of feeling everything, but you just don't feel everything all of the time. So, as much as you have **SADNESS**, you also have **HAPPINESS** in equal measure.

On a grey cloudy day, you cannot see the sun or the lovely blue sky. It is still there of course, above the clouds, but you just can't see it. When gliding through the clouds in an aeroplane, the sun is always shining and the sky is blue. We just can't see it until we rise above those clouds, but we *can* still know and remember it is still there. Connecting to both aspects allows you to be functional and feel okay. Your inner children have playmates and work together as a team and you just have to remember they are all there.

Dear Lisa

Playmates/ Counterparts

When you discover your inner children, you will be able to discover their playmates, too. At times, it is easy to see and name the playmate. Sometimes, you may find there are several playmates that can help. Some are easier to see whilst others are more difficult. Most importantly, all you need to know is that your inner children need YOU.

The list below will guide you and help you find the playmates:

Sadness	Happiness
Lack of Confidence	Confidence
Unloved	Loved
Suffering	Survival
Hate	Love
Weak	Strong
Trapped	Freedom
Afraid	Safe
Unprotected	Protected

Playmates/Counterparts

Dishonest	Honest
Lazy	Proactive
Insecure	Secure
Lack of Abundance	Abundance
Anger	Passion
Not Good Enough	Good Enough
Bad	Good
Neglected	Care
Lost	Found
Alone	Together
Unworthy	Worthy
Suicide	Life

There are many inner children. Over time, you will learn all about yours. Love them all.

Spiritual Laws

I mentioned some of the spiritual laws in my letter to Lisa.

These laws help guide us to obtain living a balanced life. The more we follow them, the more we are in control of our lives.

There is much written about the Law of Attraction and many people are aware of this law. Not so much is written about the Law of Attention, however, which personally, I feel is such an incredibly important law to know.

There are many spiritual laws, and I am going to give you a little insight to just a few of them. Diana Cooper has written a wonderful book titled, *'A Little Light on the Spiritual Laws.'* If you are interested in understanding more about the laws, this book will help.

The Law of Attention

This is such an important one. Every aspect of your life is affected and created by the level of attention you apply.

Attention is so important. How much attention are you giving? Are you giving enough? Are some areas of your life getting too much?

Spiritual Laws

If an area of your life is not running smoothly, look at the level of attention you are giving it. Things will not flourish and everything with suffer without attention.

My letter to Lisa, along with this book, is all about bringing loving attention to oneself. How much loving attention do you give yourself?

When you give attention to your feelings, you are validating them. It doesn't really matter what created them, but what does matter is what you do NOW. Giving your attention will create healing and harmony. You can't change the past, but you *are* in control of what happens now. You can make yourself feel better in every moment by giving your full attention to what you need right now.

Law of Attraction

This law works to either attract things to you or repel them away. It happens by the vibration of your energy, helping you to see what is going on inside of you. What is in your life has been attracted like a magnet to you.

As you work with the Law of *Attention*, bringing love and understanding to your inner children, you will probably find that you will attract or repel other things. As you change, so will the things and people in your life. This is one way the Law of Attention and Attraction work together.

All the laws actually work together, as do all of your inner children. Some are just more present at times than others.

Law of Perception

This one helps you become aware of how you are viewing something. Your perception is just that: YOURS.

Ten people could have a completely different view of the same situation. But whilst none of their views are either right or wrong, it will create their own reality of that situation. Each view will create a different internal reaction. Some will feel positive and some may feel negative, while others won't feel much at all.

When working with your inner children, you are using the Law of Perception to help you find the value in your uncomfortable feelings. You could perceive your pain as being negative, which will then cause you more pain. If you see that pain as a positive message to help yourself, it will ease.

In every situation, there is a valuable piece of information to learn that will help you. You would never perceive a traumatic experience as something positive, but you can *find* and *see* something positive that you can gain from having been through that experience.

So, the Law of Perception can help you grow in strength, in many ways. Just ask yourself, "How can I perceive this differently to see the positive message?"

The Law of Flow

I love this law. It always reminds me of the rivers, constantly ebbing and flowing. Water that doesn't flow starts to stagnate, so when you have flow in your life you have movement and freedom.

Spiritual Laws

When you apply this Law to your inner children you set them free from being held in the dark and locked away. When you bring loving attention to your inner children, they will be free to be with you or happily roam, only returning when they need more love.

The Law of Flow also reminds us that nothing is constant. This is helpful to remember if you are having a down-day. Our life and emotions are like a wave that we ride through our whole life. Sometimes it is gentle and calm. Sometimes the wave is strong and crashes. We are capable of riding the waves of life because we have resilience, even if at times we don't feel it.

You have survived every day of your life so far because you *do* have resilience. If you feel like you are only 'surviving' life, now, with support, you can start living your life to the full.

Law of Gratitude

There is much written about using gratitude to help with mental health. It is a very useful law to help balance your perception and feelings. It helps to reconnect you to the positive aspects that exist in your life, and helps you find them.

This is the law that your wise inner parent can use to reassure your inner children. Once you have listened to your inner children and know the loving attention they need, you can point out all the good things that exist.

If you use this law to only focus on the positive it *will* help for a while, but it may end up just distracting you from what is trying to get your attention. I know this from my own personal experience. Last year, I wrote down every day, all the things I was grateful for in my life. I have done that many times before, too. But all that did was take my attention away from the aspects of myself that needed *me*. So, I still use the Law of Gratitude but I also sit and take time to listen to my inner children.

No Outside Fix

There is nothing outside of you that can make you feel better. You can only feel better by the choices you make for yourself. You are enough and all you need, even if that means getting support from somewhere else. You will choose wisely to get the right support when you are truly being there for yourself and looking after yourself.

If you look for an outside fix in desperate need to make your pain go away, all too often you will choose something that will be unhealthy for you in the long run. You may feel momentarily better, but once the initial fix wears off you will feel much worse. Then, you will continue to search for more things to make you feel better. This cycle will just continue until you stop and look inside for what you need, and when you do this, you will prevent yourself from being manipulated or controlled in some way.

Some outside fixes may not cause you particular harm, but they won't be wholesome, and parts of you will still feel the lack. Each part wants to be fed with good wholesome food which makes you feel full and content.

To enable you to give yourself the right support, listen to what your inner children are saying, be-

Dear Lisa

cause when you listen, you understand and then know what action to take. Building a relationship with your inner children will enable you to choose healthy options and prevent you from seeking an unhealthy, outside momentary fix. The more you are there for yourself, the more your inner strength will grow and therefore enable you to choose better options.

While you are learning to be there for yourself, be aware that there may be times when you do get an outside fix. Just realise this and understand why, so it can help you chose something healthier next time. All things are a journey of learning. Changes are made through awareness and with repetition. If you don't do it the right way for you, just learn from the experience. As time goes on, it will become so much easier to do, so be gentle with yourself. In time, you will eventually learn to choose what is healthy for you.

Pain and Fear

The pain, fear and uncomfortable feelings you have, actually hold great value. These parts want to be seen, held and loved. They are held in the dark but want to be brought into the light. They are as much value to you as the parts that *do* feel comfortable. It is these parts of your inner children that will tell you what is not okay, and this valuable information enables you to make the changes so that they *do* feel okay.

When your pain or uncomfortable parts surface, ask them what is not okay for them. For example, if **NOT GOOD ENOUGH** surfaced because there is a situation where you need to achieve something or present your work, maybe in a presentation, you ask, "Why am I not feeling good enough?" The playmate counterpart is **GOOD ENOUGH** and you can use this part of yourself to support **NOT GOOD ENOUGH**. **GOOD ENOUGH** will ask, "Is there anything else that needs doing? Are you prepared and is everything ready and in place?" Together, these parts form a team. They become efficient, well prepared and get everything needed in place.

When **NOT GOOD ENOUGH** surfaces, **GOOD ENOUGH** knows how to help. The problem would be if you were disconnected to **GOOD ENOUGH**, allowing **NOT GOOD ENOUGH** to be alone in fear. Support is essential here. As soon as you feel **NOT GOOD ENOUGH**, bring in **GOOD ENOUGH** and say, "It's okay, I am here." Once they have formed a team, **GOOD ENOUGH** will present the work, but **NOT GOOD ENOUGH** will still be there, albeit feeling supported and okay.

So, **NOT GOOD ENOUGH** can serve you to either do it better or make sure everything is in place, making you even more efficient.

Personally, I have had a good connection with the positive, strong, feeling parts of myself, but I was disconnected to my pain. Having said that, I probably *was* connected to my pain, but I wasn't listening enough. I wasn't building a relationship between the different parts so they could help each other. Now that I am doing this, I feel the best I've felt in the last ten years and probably, actually, in my whole life.

I didn't need to get rid of anything. I just needed to be connected and see the value in the hurting parts of myself and learn how to love them. It is the pain that has made me feel better than I have ever felt before. I feel grounded, solid and strong. I feel so much love for all of these parts and now *all* of me feels loved, too.

Pain is often misunderstood and seen as something negative. It is actually of great benefit if the positive is found within it. Our bodies have pain receptors which alert us. For example, if we place our hand on a hot surface, we feel physical pain. The feeling of pain then causes us to take action and remove our hand. So, that pain is having a positive effect and enabling us to do something about it. If we ignored

Pain and Fear

the pain, we would cause ourselves even more harm. That is why inner pain ends up feeling so painful and awful, because it often gets ignored or buried.

Seeing the positive in listening to your pain, enables you to do something different. Understanding the benefit of pain will prevent you from rushing to distracting techniques. You will then be able to use all the wonderful, mindfulness, and positive techniques to help yourself once you understand what it is that your pain is actually telling you.

You may find it helpful not to see things as positive or negative, but instead, to see them just as they are. This can help you see the benefit in all things.

To be realistic about pain, it is never going to feel good. It is because of this, that we have to take notice of it. Imagine pain as a part of you that is shouting for you to take notice. It is what you do with the pain that then makes all the difference.

Dear Lisa

Wise Inner Parent

By listening to your inner children and understanding their needs, you will be able to develop your wise inner parent. You are basically parenting yourself, keeping yourself safe and protected, in all areas and situations of your life.

When you have a strong, wise inner parent, you will be much more able to act on your gut feelings. You will know and understand what this feeling is telling you, which will prevent you from becoming confused from all the stories your mind conjures up. Instead, you will be able to use your mind to carry out the actions needed, led by what you want from your gut feeling. This is how the head and heart work together. Your heart is what you desire and your head has the knowledge of how to achieve that.

If you are lying awake at night, trying to make sense of a situation, you have lost the connection to your gut feeling. Therefore, your mind is telling you all sorts of things as it searches for the answer. That answer lies back with your gut feeling. Reconnect with that feeling and the head will know exactly what to

Wise Inner Parent

do. It really is that simple. As soon as I catch myself trying to work out and make sense of something, I go back to what I initially felt. Instantly, I stop thinking and know exactly what I want and what action I need to take. It is very freeing and all you need to do is trust the feeling.

You will never have all the answers. But you *will* always have the answer in the present moment. You know how you feel in each moment and this is where you find the answer, an answer that will lead you on to the next step. The journey of your life will be created by each step you take NOW. Assess everything that exists right now. How do you feel? What do you need to do to achieve what is right for you?

To avoid confusion, the inner children are in your mind, but they surface from an initial gut feeling. The wise inner parent will listen to what's not feeling okay and take the positive, healthy action to bring balance. Without the wise inner parent, the child will not be able to cope, because they do not have the skills to look after themselves. All that children should be concerned about is having fun. They are carefree, full of excitement, and the magic of life, but they can only be that if they are provided with a safe, protective environment.

Dear Lisa

Self-Care Toolbox

Self-care is so important for many reasons, but essentially it is the support you give yourself on a daily basis. Daily self-care builds your resilience and your ability to cope, making you feel okay in general daily life. The stresses and trauma of everyday life can build up over time, leaving you feeling unable to cope, even with the smallest things. This is because your nervous system becomes overloaded. Your self-care will help to reduce the levels of stress that your body is holding, which actually helps you feel better physically, mentally and emotionally. There are many things you can do to calm your nervous system and support yourself.

There are three main areas to build in your self-care toolbox:

One is the support and things you can do for yourself. These are things like resting with a cup of tea if you've been busy or feel in need of a break. Have a relaxing bath. Listen to your favourite music, dance or sing. Make yourself a nice meal. Go for a lovely walk. Moisturise your skin. Make time for fun. All of

Self-Care Toolbox

these types of things are how you can support and care for yourself and meet all of your daily needs.

The second area is support you get from other people. This can include ringing a friend for a chat, maybe arranging to see a friend to do something together. Complementary therapies can work to help you stay well and offer you support. We seem to be a nation of *fix it*, rather than *look after it*. There are many different complementary therapies which help to support you physically, mentally and emotionally ones that will benefit you depending on what outcome you want. Some therapists, like myself, have lots of different skills and can adapt the treatment to help with many things. If you can't get everything you need from one therapist, have a few who can give you the treatments you want. It's very important you feel comfortable and that you trust the therapist and feel looked after by them.

The third area in the self-care toolbox is things you do with more than one other person, like group activities. This may include joining an exercise class, a walking group, a meditation group, going to a soundbath, dancing, a singing group, a craft group and things you do with like-minded people. Connecting with others, in an activity you enjoy, allows for everyone to benefit from the wisdom of each person, because sharing and listening to each other creates a sense of community and belonging.

There are many things you can put into your self-care toolbox, but most importantly, they are all the things that work for you. Bring out the one you need when it's the right one for that moment or day.

Journaling

Journaling is a useful way to help you express what you are feeling. You can journal every day or just when you feel the need to take some time to reflect on something.

Always put the date when writing something down, as this helps to see how your journey evolves. As you write and express how you are feeling, the connection to yourself will grow and will help you to see your inner children. Journaling is a good tool to help you listen to what they are saying.

Once you have written down what you feel, write down what you need and what you can then do. This helps you to be connected to yourself and thereby stay connected.

You may want to draw illustrations in your journal, write poems or letters to yourself or others, and perhaps write inspirational messages.

Journals are very personal, and there are lovely journaling books available, too. You may even want to get yourself a special journaling pen.

It's Okay Not to Feel Okay

There will be times in your life where you simply will not feel okay, and that, in itself, *is* okay.

You are human, full of different emotions and occasionally, these emotions, which we can see as inner children, will surface.

They will be present in many different situations, such as the following:

Bereavement

Illness

Menopause

Divorce and separation

Career issues

Pregnancy

Childbirth

Abuse

Relationship issues

Family issues

Dear Lisa

Many different situations can cause you not to feel okay and sometimes you will just have an off-day. You can be influenced by so many things around you and within you. Some you can control but others you can't, like, for example, the effects of hormones fluctuating. What you *can* do is understand it is okay *not* to feel okay. With your wise inner parent, you will be able to look after yourself, giving yourself a safe space to be in until you feel okay again.

Whatever the situation, however you feel, always remember to look after yourself.

Final Note

You have now seen how to love and be there for yourself. When you embrace all these aspects and see their value, you will feel lighter and freer. You are now saying to yourself, "I value you; I respect you; I see your worth; you are important." And, importantly, "I love you." You are acknowledging all parts of your whole self and treating them as equals. This is what being whole feels like. Treating yourself in this way is kind and loving, and *all* of you will feel loved.

Remember, you are not broken nor do you need fixing. You just want to be loved, as do we all. There is nothing wrong with you if you are having a bad day, because simply, you are just having a bad day. You don't even need more healing; you just need to look after yourself. You know how to do that, now. Use this book to remind you and keep you focused, and with time you will find being there for yourself so much easier to do. It will eventually feel so natural but do allow yourself time. Everything evolves over time. Be proactive and give yourself a moment to listen so you can give yourself the healthy, loving attention that you need.

Stop
Listen
Communicate
Give Loving Attention
Take action or give reassurance
Your needs are now met

Dear Lisa

Acknowledgments

I would like to thank Karen, my dear friend and client, for reading my very first draft. I'm so grateful to have received such valuable guidance which enabled me to learn and make the necessary improvements.

I would also like to thank my friends who gave me such valuable feedback. Hearing how my story and the discovery of my inner children has help each one in some way, gave me such encouragement.

I would like to thank my friend, Sharon, for proof reading and highlighting so clearly where I needed to make corrections.

I feel it's important to give thanks to everyone I have written about. Each person, each situation, has given me an opportunity to discover another inner child and be able to love myself more.

I want to thank myself and my inner children for never giving up. I'm grateful I always hold great compassion for myself and others.

I am so grateful to everyone who has supported me in some way, from the very beginning, even before writing a single word, to finding my editor, Kathryn Hall.

Acknowledgments

I would like to thank Kathryn for so much more than editing my book. I really appreciated being kept informed every step of the way. I was so excited after receiving such wonderful feedback about the impact my book had on her understanding the inner children. It's wonderful to work with someone who is present, efficient, encouraging and caring.

Finally, I'd like to that Hammad Khalid for formatting and designing the beautiful cover.

Dear Lisa

Resources

Facebook - Anji Marsh

Contact Anji for Email Inner Children Coaching and Self-Awareness Mentoring

Email
anjimarsh68@gmail.com

NO HANDS® Massage
https://nohandsmassage.com

Diana Cooper
https://dianacooper.com

Emmett UK
https://www.emmett-uk.co.uk/

Life Without a Centre – Jeff Foster
https://www.lifewithoutacentre.com

Printed in Great Britain
by Amazon